John James Audubon

by

John Burroughs

AF729084

Double 9 BOOKS

John James Audubon

by John Burroughs

Copyright © 2024

All Rights reserved.

No part of this publication may be reproduced, stored in a retrieval system, or transmitted in any form or by any means, electronic, mechanical, photocopying or Otherwise, without the written permission of the publisher.
The author/editor asserts the moral right to be identified as the author/editor of this work.

ISBN: 978-93-62769-28-2

Published by

DOUBLE 9 BOOKS
2/13-B, Ansari Road
Daryaganj, New Delhi – 110002
info@double9books.com
www.double9books.com
Tel. 011-40042856

This book is under public domain

ABOUT THE AUTHOR

John Burroughs was an American naturalist and nature essayist who lived from April 3, 1837, to March 29, 1921. He was involved in the conservation movement in the US. His first book of essays, Wake-Robin, came out in 1871. His biographer, Edward Renehan, said that Burroughs wasn't really a scientific naturalist. Instead, he was a literary naturalist with a duty to record his own unique perceptions of the natural world." The result was a body of work that fit perfectly with the mood of its time, which is why it was so famous at the time and not so well known since then. Burroughs was the seventh child of Chauncy Burroughs and Amy Kelly. He was born in Delaware County, New York, on the family farm in the Catskill Mountains, close to Roxbury. As a child, he spent a lot of time on the slopes of Old Clump Mountain, where he could see the higher peaks of the Catskills, especially Slide Mountain, which he would write about later. He worked hard on the family farm and was amazed by the birds that came back every spring and the other animals that lived near the farm, like frogs and bumblebees.

CONTENTS

PREFACE

The pioneer in American ornithology was Alexander Wilson, a Scotch weaver and poet, who emigrated to this country in 1794, and began the publication of his great work upon our birds in 1808. He figured and described three hundred and twenty species, fifty-six of them new to science. His death occurred in 1813, before the publication of his work had been completed.

But the chief of American ornithologists was John James Audubon. Audubon did not begin where Wilson left off. He was also a pioneer, beginning his studies and drawings of the birds probably as early as Wilson did his, but he planned larger and lived longer. He spent the greater part of his long life in the pursuit of ornithology, and was of a more versatile, flexible, and artistic nature than was Wilson. He was collecting the material for his work at the same time that Wilson was collecting his, but he did not begin the publication of it till fourteen years after Wilson's death. Both men went directly to Nature and underwent incredible hardships in exploring the woods and marshes in quest of their material. Audubon's rambles were much wider, and extended over a much longer period of time. Wilson, too, contemplated a work upon our quadrupeds, but did not live to begin it. Audubon was blessed with good health, length of years, a devoted and self-sacrificing wife, and a buoyant, sanguine, and elastic disposition. He had the heavenly gift of enthusiasm—a passionate love for the work he set out to do. He was a natural hunter, roamer, woodsman; as unworldly as a child, and as simple and transparent. We have had better trained and more scientific ornithologists since his day, but none with his abandon and poetic fervour in the study of our birds.

Both men were famous pedestrians and often walked hundreds of miles at a stretch. They were natural explorers and voyagers. They loved Nature at first hand, and not merely as she appears in books and pictures. They both kept extensive journals of their wanderings and observations. Several of Audubon's (recording his European experiences) seem to have been lost or destroyed, but what remain make up the greater part of two large volumes recently edited by his grand-daughter, Maria R. Audubon.

I wish here to express my gratitude both to Miss Audubon, and to Messrs. Charles Scribner's Sons, for permitting me to draw freely from the "Life and Journals" just mentioned. The temptation is strong to let Audubon's graphic and glowing descriptions of American scenery, and of his tireless wanderings, speak for themselves.

It is from these volumes, and from the life by his widow, published in 1868, that I have gathered the material for this brief biography.

Audubon's life naturally divides itself into three periods: his youth, which was on the whole a gay and happy one, and which lasted till the time of his marriage at the age of twenty-eight; his business career which followed, lasting ten or more years, and consisting mainly in getting rid of the fortune his father had left him; and his career as an ornithologist which, though attended with great hardships and privations, brought him much happiness and, long before the end, substantial pecuniary rewards.

His ornithological tastes and studies really formed the main current of his life from his teens onward. During his business ventures in Kentucky and elsewhere this current came to the surface more and more, absorbed more and more of his time and energies, and carried him further and further from the conditions of a successful business career.

J. B.
WEST PARK, NEW YORK, January, 1902.

CHRONOLOGY

1780

May 4. John James La Forest Audubon was born at Mandeville, Louisiana.

(Paucity of dates and conflicting statements make it impossible to insert dates to show when the family moved to St. Domingo, and thence to France.)

1797 (?)

Returned to America from France. Here followed life at Mill Grove Farm, near Philadelphia.

1805 or 6

Again in France for about two years. Studied under David, the artist. Then returned to America.

1808

April 8. Married Lucy Bakewell, and journeyed to Louisville, Kentucky, to engage in business with one Rozier.

1810

March. First met Wilson, the ornithologist.

1812

Dissolved partnership with Rozier.

1808-1819

Various business ventures in Louisville, Hendersonville, and St. Geneviève, Kentucky, again at Hendersonville, thence again to Louisville.

1819

Abandoned business career. Became taxidermist in Cincinnati.

1820

Left Cincinnati. Began to form definite plans for the publication of his drawings. Returned to New Orleans.

1822

Went to Natchez by steamer. Gunpowder ruined two hundred of his drawings on this trip. Obtained position of Drawing-master in the college at Washington, Mississippi. At the close of this year took his first lessons in oils.

1824

Went to Philadelphia to get his drawings published. Thwarted. There met Sully, and Prince Canino.

1826

Sailed for Europe to introduce his drawings.

1827

Issued prospectus of his "Birds."

1828

Went to Paris to canvass. Visited Cuvier.

1829

Returned to the United States, scoured the woods for more material for his biographies.

1830

Returned to London with his family.

1830-1839

Elephant folio, *The Birds of North America*, published.

1831-39

American Ornithological Biography published in Edinburgh.

1831

Again in America for nearly three years.

1832-33

In Florida, South Carolina, and the Northern States, Labrador, and Canada.

1834

Completion of second volume of "Birds," also second volume of *American Ornithological Biography*.

1835

In Edinburgh.

1836

To New York again—more exploring; found books, papers and drawings had been destroyed by fire, the previous year.

1837

Went to London.

1838

Published fourth volume of *American Ornithological Biography*.

1839

Published fifth volume of "Biography."

1840

Left England for the last time.

1842

Built house in New York on "Minnie's Land," now Audubon Park.

1843

Yellowstone River Expedition.

1840-44

Published the reduced edition of his "Bird Biographies."

1846

Published first volume of "Quadrupeds."

1848

Completed *Quadrupeds and Biography of American Quadrupeds*. (The last volume was not published till 1854, after his death.)

1851

January 27. John James Audubon died in New York.

JOHN JAMES AUDUBON

I

There is a hopeless confusion as to certain important dates in Audubon's life. He was often careless and unreliable in his statements of matters of fact, which weakness during his lifetime often led to his being accused of falsehood. Thus he speaks of the "memorable battle of Valley Forge" and of two brothers of his, both officers in the French army, as having perished in the French Revolution, when he doubtless meant uncles. He had previously stated that his only two brothers died in infancy. He confessed that he had no head for mathematics, and he seems always to have been at sea in regard to his own age. In his letters and journals there are several references to his age, but they rarely agree. The date of his birth usually given, May 4, 1780, is probably three or four years too early, as he speaks of himself as being nearly seventeen when his mother had him confirmed in the Catholic Church, and this was about the time that his father, then an officer in the French navy, was sent to England to effect a change of prisoners, which time is given as 1801.

The two race strains that mingle in him probably account for this illogical habit of mind, as well as for his romantic and artistic temper and tastes.

His father was a sea-faring man and a Frenchman; his mother was a Spanish Creole of Louisiana—the old chivalrous Castilian blood modified by new world conditions. The father, through commercial channels, accumulated a large property in the island of St. Domingo. In the course of his trading he made frequent journeys to Louisiana, then the property of the French government. On one of these trips, probably, he married one of the native women, who is said to have possessed both wealth and beauty. The couple seem to have occupied for a time a plantation belonging to a French Marquis, situated at Mandeville on the North shore of Lake Pontchartrain. Here three sons were born to them, of whom John James La Forest was the third. The daughter seems to have been younger.

His own mother perished in a slave insurrection in St. Domingo, where the family had gone to live on the Audubon estate at Aux Cayes, when her child was but a few months old. Audubon says that his father with his plate and money and himself, attended by a few faithful servants, escaped to New Orleans. What became of his sister he does not say, though she must have escaped with them, since we hear of her existence years later. Not long after, how long we do not know, the father returned to France, where he married a second time, giving the son, as he himself says, the only mother he ever knew. This woman proved a rare exception among stepmothers—but she was too indulgent, and, Audubon says, completely spoiled him, bringing him up to live like a gentleman, ignoring his faults and boasting of his merits, and leading him to believe that fine clothes and a full pocket were the most desirable things in life.

This she was able to do all the more effectively because the father soon left the son in her charge and returned to the United States in the employ of the French government, and before long became attached to the army under La Fayette. This could not have been later than 1781, the year of Cornwallis' surrender, and Audubon would then have been twenty-one, but this does not square with his own statements. After the war the father still served some years in the French navy, but finally retired from active service and lived at La Gerbétière in France, where he died at the age of ninety-five, in 1818.

Audubon says of his mother: "Let no one speak of her as my step-mother. I was ever to her as a son of her own flesh and blood and she was to me a true mother." With her he lived in the city of Nantes, France, where he appears to have gone to school. It was, however, only from his private tutors that he says he got any benefit. His father desired him to follow in his footsteps, and he was educated accordingly, studying drawing, geography, mathematics, fencing, and music. Mathematics he found hard dull work, as have so many men of like temperament, before and since, but music and fencing and geography were more to his liking. He was an ardent, imaginative youth, and chafed under all drudgery and routine. His foster-mother, in the absence of his father, suffered him to do much as he pleased, and he pleased to "play hookey" most of the time, joining boys of his own age and disposition, and deserting the school for the fields and woods, hunting birds' nests, fishing and shooting and returning home at night with his basket filled with various natural specimens and curiosities. The collecting fever is not a bad one to take possession of boys at this age.

In his autobiography Audubon relates an incident that occurred when he was a child, which he thinks first kindled his love for birds. It was an encounter between a pet parrot and a tame monkey kept by his mother. One morning the parrot, Mignonne, asked as usual for her breakfast of bread and milk, whereupon the monkey, being in a bad humour, attacked the poor defenceless bird, and killed it. Audubon screamed at the cruel sight, and implored the servant to interfere and save the bird, but without avail. The boy's piercing screams brought the mother, who succeeded in tranquillising the child. The monkey was chained, and the parrot buried, but the tragedy awakened in him a lasting love for his feathered friends.

Audubon's father seems to have been the first to direct his attention to the study of birds, and to the observance of Nature generally. Through him he learned to notice the beautiful colourings and markings of the birds, to know their haunts, and to observe their change of plumage with the changing seasons; what he learned of their mysterious migrations fired his imagination.

He speaks of this early intimacy with Nature as a feeling which bordered on frenzy. Watching the growth of a bird from the egg he compares to the unfolding of a flower from the bud.

The pain which he felt in seeing the birds die and decay was very acute, but, fortunately, about this time some one showed him a book of illustrations, and henceforth "a new life ran in my veins," he says. To copy Nature was thereafter his one engrossing aim.

That he realised how crude his early efforts were is shown by his saying: "My pencil gave birth to a family of cripples." His steady progress, too, is shown in his custom, on every birthday, of burning these 'Crippled' drawings, then setting to work to make better, truer ones.

His father returning from a sea voyage, probably when the son was about twenty years old, was not well pleased with the progress that the boy was making in his studies. One morning soon after, Audubon found himself with his trunk and his belongings in a private carriage, beside his father, on his way to the city of Rochefort. The father occupied himself with a book and hardly spoke to his son during the several days of the journey, though there was no anger in his face. After they were settled in their new abode, he seated his son beside him and taking one of his hands in his, calmly said: "My beloved boy, thou art now safe. I have brought thee here that I may be able to pay constant attention to thy studies; thou shalt have ample time for pleasures, but the remainder *must* be employed with industry and care."

But the father soon left him on some foreign mission for his government and the boy chafed as usual under his tasks and confinement. One day, too much mathematics drove him into making his escape by leaping from the window, and making off through the gardens attached to the school where he was confined. A watchful corporal soon overhauled him, however, and brought him back, where he was confined on board some sort of prison ship in the harbour. His father soon returned, when he was released, not without a severe reprimand.

We next find him again in the city of Nantes struggling with more odious mathematics, and spending all his leisure time in the fields and woods, studying the birds. About this time he began a series of drawings of the French birds, which grew to upwards of two hundred, all bad enough, he says, but yet real representations of birds, that gave him a certain pleasure. They satisfied his need of expression.

At about this time, too, though the year we do not know, his father concluded to send him to the United States, apparently to occupy a farm called Mill Grove, which the father had purchased some years before, on the Schuylkill river near Philadelphia. In New York he caught the yellow fever: he was carefully nursed by two Quaker ladies who kept a boarding house in Morristown, New Jersey.

In due time his father's agent, Miers Fisher, also a Quaker, removed him to his own villa near Philadelphia, and here Audubon seems to have remained some months. But the gay and ardent youth did not find the atmosphere of the place congenial. The sober Quaker grey was not to his taste. His host was opposed to music of all kinds, and to dancing, hunting, fishing and nearly all other forms of amusement. More than that, he had a daughter between whom and Audubon he apparently hoped an affection would spring up. But Audubon took an unconquerable dislike to her. Very soon, therefore, he demanded to be put in possession of the estate to which his father had sent him.

Of the month and year in which he entered upon his life at Mill Grove, we are ignorant. We know that he fell into the hands of another Quaker, William Thomas, who was the tenant on the place, but who, with his worthy wife, seems to have made life pleasant for him. He soon became attached to Mill Grove, and led a life there just suited to his temperament.

"Hunting, fishing, drawing, music, occupied my every moment; cares I knew not and cared naught about them. I purchased excellent and beautiful horses, visited all such neighbours as I found congenial spirits, and was as happy as happy could be."

Near him there lived an English family by the name of Bakewell, but he had such a strong antipathy to the English that he postponed returning the call of Mr. Bakewell, who had left his card at Mill Grove during one of Audubon's excursions to the woods. In the late fall or early winter, however, he chanced to meet Mr. Bakewell while out hunting grouse, and was so pleased with him and his well-trained dogs, and his good marksmanship, that he apologised for his discourtesy in not returning his call, and promised to do so forthwith. Not many mornings thereafter he was seated in his neighbour's house.

"Well do I recollect the morning," he says in the autobiographical sketch which he prepared for his sons, "and may it please God that I never forget it, when for the first time I entered Mr. Bakewell's dwelling. It happened that he was absent from home, and I was shown into a parlour where only one young lady was snugly seated at her work by the fire. She rose on my entrance, offered me a seat, assured me of the gratification her father would feel on his return, which, she added, would be in a few moments, as she would despatch a servant for him. Other ruddy cheeks and bright eyes made their transient appearance, but, like spirits gay, soon vanished from my sight; and there I sat, my gaze riveted, as it were, on the young girl before me, who, half working, half talking, essayed to make the time pleasant to me. Oh! may God bless her! It was she, my dear sons, who afterwards became my beloved wife, and your mother. Mr. Bakewell soon made his appearance, and received me with the manner and hospitality of a true English gentleman. The other members of the family were soon introduced to me, and Lucy was told to have luncheon produced. She now rose from her seat a second time, and her form, to which I had paid but partial attention, showed both grace and beauty; and my heart followed every one of her steps. The repast over, dogs and guns were made ready.

"Lucy, I was pleased to believe, looked upon me with some favour, and I turned more especially to her on leaving. I felt that certain '*Je ne sais quoi*' which intimated that, at least, she was not indifferent to me."

The winter that followed was a gay and happy one at Mill Grove; shooting parties, skating parties, house parties with the Bakewell family, were of frequent occurrence. It was during one of these skating excursions upon the Perkiomen in quest of wild ducks, that Audubon had a lucky escape from drowning. He was leading the party down the river in the dusk of the evening, with a white handkerchief tied to a stick, when he came suddenly upon a large air hole into which, in spite of himself, his impetus carried him. Had there not chanced to be another air hole a few yards below, our hero's career would have ended then and there. The current quickly carried him beneath the ice to this other opening where he managed to seize hold of the ice and to crawl out.

His friendship with the Bakewell family deepened. Lucy taught Audubon English, he taught her drawing, and their friendship very naturally ripened into love, which seems to have run its course smoothly.

Audubon was happy. He had ample means, and his time was filled with congenial pursuits. He writes in his journal: "I had no vices, but was thoughtless, pensive, loving, fond of shooting, fishing, and riding, and had a passion for raising all sorts of fowls, which sources of interest and amusement fully occupied my time. It was one of my fancies to be ridiculously fond of dress; to hunt in black satin breeches, wear pumps when shooting, and to dress in the finest ruffled shirts I could obtain from France."

The evidences of vanity regarding his looks and apparel, sometimes found in his journal, are probably traceable to his foster-mother's unwise treatment of him in his youth. We have seen how his father's intervention in the nick of time exercised a salutary influence upon him at this point in his career, directing his attention to the more solid attainments. Whatever traces of this self-consciousness and apparent vanity remained in after life, seem to have been more the result of a naïve character delighting in picturesqueness in himself as well as in Nature, than they were of real vanity.

In later years he was assuredly nothing of the dandy; he himself ridicules his youthful fondness for dress, while those who visited him during his last years speak of him as particularly lacking in self-consciousness.

Although he affected the dress of the dandies of his time, he was temperate and abstemious. "I ate no butcher's meat, lived chiefly on fruits, vegetables, and fish, and never drank a glass of spirits or wine until my wedding day." "All this time I was fair and rosy, strong and active as one of my age and sex could be, and as active and agile as a buck."

That he was energetic and handy and by no means the mere dandy that his extravagance in dress might seem to indicate, is evidenced from the fact that about this time he made a journey on foot to New York and accomplished the ninety miles in three days in mid-winter. But he was angry, and anger is better than wine to walk on.

The cause of his wrath was this; a lead mine had been discovered upon the farm of Mill Grove, and Audubon had applied to his father for counsel in regard to it. In response, the elder Audubon had sent over a man by the name of Da Costa who was to act as his son's partner and partial guardian—was to teach him mineralogy and mining engineering, and to look after his finances generally. But the man, Audubon says, knew nothing of the subjects he was supposed to teach, and was, besides, "a covetous wretch, who did all he could to ruin my father, and, indeed, swindled both of us to a large amount." Da Costa pushed his authority so far as to object to Audubon's proposed union with Lucy Bakewell, as being a marriage beneath him, and finally plotted to get the young man off to India. These things very naturally kindled Audubon's quick temper, and he demanded of his tutor and guardian money enough to take him to France to consult with his father. Da Costa gave him a letter of credit on a sort of banker-broker residing in New York. To New York he accordingly went, as above stated, and found that the banker-broker was in the plot to pack him off to India. This disclosure kindled his wrath afresh. He says that had he had a weapon about him the banker's heart must have received the result of his wrath. His Spanish blood began to declare itself.

Then he sought out a brother of Mr. Bakewell and the uncle of his sweetheart, and of him borrowed the money to take him to France. He took passage on a New Bedford brig bound for Nantes. The captain had recently been married and when the vessel reached the vicinity of New Bedford, he discovered some dangerous leaks which necessitated a week's delay to repair damages. Audubon avers that the captain had caused holes to be bored in the vessel's sides below the water line, to gain an excuse to spend a few more days with his bride.

After a voyage of nineteen days the vessel entered the Loire, and anchored in the lower harbour of Nantes, and Audubon was soon welcomed by his father and fond foster-mother.

His first object was to have the man Da Costa disposed of, which he soon accomplished; the second, to get his father's consent to his marriage with Lucy Bakewell, which was also brought about in due time, although the parents of both agreed that they were "owre young to marry yet."

Audubon now remained two years in France, indulging his taste for hunting, rambling, and drawing birds and other objects of Natural History.

This was probably about the years 1805 and 1806. France was under the sway of Napoleon, and conscriptions were the order of the day. The elder Audubon became uneasy lest his son be drafted into the French army; hence he resolved to send him back to America. In the meantime, he interested one Rozier in the lead mine and had formed a partnership between him and his son, to run for nine years. In due course the two young men sailed for New York, leaving France at a time when thousands would have been glad to have followed their footsteps.

On this voyage their vessel was pursued and overhauled by a British privateer, the *Rattlesnake*, and nearly all their money and eatables were carried off, besides two of the ship's best sailors. Audubon and Rozier saved their gold by hiding it under a cable in the bow of the ship.

On returning to Mill Grove, Audubon resumed his former habits of life there. We hear no more of the lead mine, but more of his bird studies and drawings, the love of which was fast becoming his ruling passion. "Before I sailed for France, I had begun a series of drawings of the birds of America, and had also begun a study of their habits. I at first drew my subject dead, by which I mean to say that after procuring a specimen, I hung it up, either by the head, wing, or foot, and copied it as closely as I could." Even the hateful Da Costa had praised his bird pictures and had predicted great things for him in this direction. His words had given Audubon a great deal of pleasure.

Mr. William Bakewell, the brother of his Lucy, has given us a glimpse of Audubon and his surroundings at this time. "Audubon took me to his house, where he and his companion, Rozier, resided, with Mrs. Thomas for an attendant. On entering his room, I was astonished and delighted that it was turned into a museum. The walls were festooned with all sorts of birds' eggs, carefully blown out and strung on a thread. The chimney piece was covered with stuffed squirrels, raccoons and opossums; and the shelves around were likewise crowded with specimens, among which were fishes, frogs, snakes, lizards, and other reptiles. Besides these stuffed varieties, many paintings were arrayed upon the walls, chiefly of birds. He had great skill in stuffing and preserving animals of all sorts. He had also a trick of training dogs with great perfection, of which art his famous dog Zephyr was a wonderful example. He was an admirable marksman, an expert swimmer, a clever rider, possessed great activity, prodigious strength, and was notable for the elegance of his figure, and the beauty of his features, and he aided Nature by a careful attendance to his dress. Besides other accomplishments, he was musical, a good fencer, danced well, had some acquaintance with legerdemain tricks, worked in hair, and could plait willow baskets." He adds that Audubon once swam across the Schuylkill with him on his back.

II

Audubon was now eager to marry, but Mr. Bakewell advised him first to study the mercantile business. This he accordingly set out to do by entering as a clerk the commercial house of Benjamin Bakewell in New York, while his friend Rozier entered a French house in Philadelphia.

But Audubon was not cut out for business; his first venture was in indigo, and cost him several hundred pounds. Rozier succeeded no better; his first speculation was a cargo of hams shipped to the West Indies which did not return one fifth of the cost. Audubon's want of business habits is shown by the statement that at this time he one day posted a letter containing eight thousand dollars without sealing it. His heart was in the fields and woods with the birds. His room was filled with drying bird skins, the odour from which, it is said, became so strong that his neighbours sent a constable to him with a message to abate the nuisance.

Despairing of becoming successful business men in either New York or Philadelphia, he and Rozier soon returned to Mill Grove. During some of their commercial enterprises they had visited Kentucky and thought so well of the outlook there that now their thoughts turned thitherward.

Here we get the first date from Audubon; on April 8, 1808, he and Lucy Bakewell were married. The plantation of Mill Grove had been previously sold, and the money invested in goods with which to open a store in Louisville, Kentucky. The day after the marriage, Audubon and his wife and Mr. Rozier started on their journey. In crossing the mountains to Pittsburg the coach in which they were travelling upset, and Mrs. Audubon was severely bruised. From Pittsburg they floated down the Ohio in a flatboat in company with several other young emigrant families. The voyage occupied twelve days and was no doubt made good use of by Audubon in observing the wild nature along shore.

In Louisville, he and Rozier opened a large store which promised well. But Audubon's heart was more and more with the birds, and his business more and more neglected. Rozier attended to the counter, and, Audubon says, grew rich, but he himself spent most of the time in the woods or hunting with the planters settled about Louisville, between whom and himself a warm attachment soon sprang up. He was not growing rich, but he was happy. "I shot, I drew, I looked on Nature only," he says, "and my days were happy beyond human conception, and beyond this I really cared not."

He says that the only part of the commercial business he enjoyed was the ever engaging journeys which he made to New York and Philadelphia to purchase goods.

These journeys led him through the "beautiful, the darling forests of Ohio, Kentucky, and Pennsylvania," and on one occasion he says he lost sight of the pack horses carrying his goods and his dollars, in his preoccupation with a new warbler.

During his residence in Louisville, Alexander Wilson, his great rival in American ornithology, called upon him. This is Audubon's account of the meeting: "One fair morning I was surprised by the sudden entrance into our counting room at Louisville of Mr. Alexander Wilson, the celebrated author of the American Ornithology, of whose existence I had never until that moment been apprised. This happened in March, 1810. How well do I remember him as he then walked up to me. His long, rather hooked nose, the keenness of his eyes, and his prominent cheek bones, stamped his countenance with a peculiar character. His dress, too, was of a kind not usually seen in that part of the country; a short coat, trousers and a waistcoat of grey cloth. His stature was not above the middle size. He had two volumes under his arm, and as he approached the table at which I was working, I thought I discovered something like astonishment in his countenance. He, however, immediately proceeded to disclose the object of his visit, which was to procure subscriptions for his work. He opened his books, explained the nature of his occupations, and requested my patronage. I felt surprised and gratified at the sight of his volumes, turned over a few of the plates, and had already taken my pen to write my name in his favour, when my partner rather abruptly said to me in French: 'My dear Audubon, what induces you to subscribe to this work! Your drawings are certainly far better; and again, you must know as much of the habits of American birds as this gentleman.' Whether Mr. Wilson understood French or not, or if the suddenness with which I paused disappointed him, I cannot tell; but I clearly perceived he was not pleased. Vanity, and the encomiums of my friend, prevented me from subscribing. Mr. Wilson asked me if I had many drawings of birds, I rose, took down a large portfolio, laid it on the table, and showed him as I would show you, kind reader, or any other person fond of such subjects, the whole of the contents, with the same patience, with which he had showed me his own engravings. His surprise appeared great, as he told me he had never had the most distant idea that any other individual than himself had been engaged in forming such a collection. He asked me if it was my intention to publish, and when I answered in the negative, his surprise seemed to increase. And, truly, such was not my intention; for, until long after, when I met the Prince of Musignano in Philadelphia, I had not the least idea of presenting the fruits of my labours to the world. Mr. Wilson now examined my drawings with care, asked if I should have any objection to lending him a few during his stay, to which I replied that I had none. He then bade me good morning, not, however, until I had made an arrangement to explore the woods in the vicinity along with him, and had promised to procure for him some birds, of which I had drawings in my collection, but which he had never seen. It happened that he lodged in the same house with us, but his retired habits, I thought, exhibited a strong feeling of discontent, or a decided melancholy. The Scotch airs which he played sweetly on his flute made me melancholy, too, and I felt for him. I presented him to my wife and friends, and seeing that he was all enthusiasm, exerted myself as much as was in my power to procure for him the specimens which he wanted.

"We hunted together and obtained birds which he had never before seen; but, reader, I did not subscribe to his work, for, even at that time, my collection was greater than his.

"Thinking that perhaps he might be pleased to publish the results of my researches, I offered them to him, merely on condition that what I had drawn, or might afterward draw and send to him, should be mentioned in his work as coming from my pencil. I at the same time offered to open a correspondence with him, which I thought might prove beneficial to us both. He made no reply to either proposal, and before many days had elapsed, left Louisville on his way to New Orleans, little knowing how much his talents were appreciated in our little town, at least by myself and my friends."

Wilson's account of this meeting is in curious contrast to that of Audubon. It is meagre and unsatisfactory. Under date of March 19, he writes in his diary at Louisville: "Rambled around the town with my gun. Examined Mr. ——'s [Audubon's] drawings in crayons—very good. Saw two new birds he had, both *Motacillae*."

March 21. "Went out this afternoon shooting with Mr. A. Saw a number of Sandhill cranes. Pigeons numerous."

Finally, in winding up the record of his visit to Louisville, he says, with palpable inconsistency, not to say falsehood, that he did not receive one act of civility there, nor see one new bird, and found no naturalist to keep him company.

Some years afterward, Audubon hunted him up in Philadelphia, and found him drawing a white headed eagle. He was civil, and showed Audubon some attention, but "spoke not of birds or drawings."

Wilson was of a nature far less open and generous than was Audubon. It is evident that he looked upon the latter as his rival, and was jealous of his superior talents; for superior they were in many ways. Audubon's drawings have far more spirit and artistic excellence, and his text shows far more enthusiasm and hearty affiliation with Nature. In accuracy of observation, Wilson is fully his equal, if not his superior.

As Audubon had deserted his business, his business soon deserted him; he and his partner soon became discouraged (we hear no more about the riches Rozier had acquired), and resolved upon moving their goods to Hendersonville, Kentucky, over one hundred miles further down the Ohio. Mrs. Audubon and her baby son were sent back to her father's at Fatland Ford where they remained upwards of a year.

Business at Hendersonville proved dull; the country was but thinly inhabited and only the coarsest goods were in demand. To procure food the merchants had to resort to fishing and hunting. They employed a clerk who proved a good shot; he and Audubon supplied the table while Rozier again stood behind the counter.

How long the Hendersonville enterprise lasted we do not know. Another change was finally determined upon, and the next glimpse we get of Audubon, we see him with his clerk and partner and their remaining stock in trade, consisting of three hundred barrels of whiskey, sundry dry goods and powder, on board a keel boat making their way down the Ohio, in a severe snow storm, toward St. Geneviève, a settlement on the Mississippi River, where they proposed to try again. The boat is steered by a long oar, about sixty feet in length, made of the trunk of a slender tree, and shaped at its outer extremity like the fin of a dolphin; four oars in the bow propelled her, and with the current they made about five miles an hour.

Mrs. Audubon, who seems to have returned from her father's, with her baby, or babies, was left behind at Hendersonville with a friend, until the result of the new venture should be determined.

In the course of six weeks, after many delays, and adventures with the ice and the cold, the party reached St. Geneviève.

Audubon has given in his journal a very vivid and interesting account of this journey. At St. Geneviève, the whiskey was in great demand, and what had cost them twenty-five cents a gallon, was sold for two dollars. But Audubon soon became discouraged with the place and longed to be back in Hendersonville with his family. He did not like the low bred French-Canadians, who made up most of the population of the settlement. He sold out his interest in the business to his partner, who liked the place and the people, and here the two parted company. Audubon purchased a fine horse and started over the prairies on his return trip to Hendersonville.

On this journey he came near being murdered by a woman and her two desperate sons who lived in a cabin on the prairies, where the traveller put up for the night. He has given a minute and graphic account of this adventure in his journal.

The cupidity of the woman had been aroused by the sight of Audubon's gold watch and chain. A wounded Indian, who had also sought refuge in the shanty had put Audubon upon his guard. It was midnight, Audubon lay on some bear skins in one corner of the room, feigning sleep. He had previously slipped out of the cabin and had loaded his gun, which lay close at hand. Presently he saw the woman sharpen a huge carving knife, and thrust it into the hand of her drunken son, with the injunction to kill yon stranger and secure the watch. He was just on the point of springing up to shoot his would-be murderers, when the door burst open, and two travellers, each with a long knife, appeared. Audubon jumped up and told them his situation. The drunken sons and the woman were bound, and in the morning they were taken out into the woods and were treated as the Regulators treated delinquents in those days. They were shot. Whether Audubon did any of the shooting or not, he does not say. But he aided and abetted, and his Spanish blood must have tingled in his veins. Then the cabin was set on fire, and the travellers proceeded on their way.

It must be confessed that this story sounds a good deal like an episode in a dime novel, and may well be taken with a grain of allowance. Did remote prairie cabins in those days have grindstones and carving knives? And why should the would-be murderers use a knife when they had guns?

Audubon reached Hendersonville in early March, and witnessed the severe earthquake which visited that part of Kentucky the following November, 1812. Of this experience we also have a vivid account in his journals.

Audubon continued to live at Hendersonville, his pecuniary means much reduced. He says that he made a pedestrian tour back to St. Geneviève to collect money due him from Rozier, walking the one hundred and sixty-five miles, much of the time nearly ankle-deep in mud and water, in a little over three days. Concerning the accuracy of this statement one also has his doubts. Later he bought a "wild horse," and on its back travelled over Tennessee and a portion of Georgia, and so around to Philadelphia, later returning to Hendersonville.

He continued his drawings of birds and animals, but, in the meantime, embarked in another commercial venture, and for a time prospered. Some years previously he had formed a co-partnership with his wife's brother, and a commercial house in charge of Bakewell had been opened in New Orleans. This turned out disastrously and was a constant drain upon his resources.

This partner now appears upon the scene at Hendersonville and persuades Audubon to erect, at a heavy outlay, a steam grist and saw mill, and to take into the firm an Englishman by the name of Pease.

This enterprise brought fresh disaster. "How I laboured at this infernal mill, from dawn till dark, nay, at times all night."

They also purchased a steamboat which was so much additional weight to drag them down. This was about the year 1817. From this date till 1819, Audubon's pecuniary difficulties increased daily. He had no business talent whatever; he was a poet and an artist; he cared not for money, he wanted to be alone with Nature. The forests called to him, the birds haunted his dreams.

His father dying in 1818, left him a valuable estate in France, and seventeen thousand dollars, deposited with a merchant in Richmond, Virginia; but Audubon was so dilatory in proving his identity and his legal right to this cash, that the merchant finally died insolvent, and the legatee never received a cent of it. The French estate he transferred in after years to his sister Rosa.

III

Finally, Audubon gave up the struggle of trying to be a business man. He says: "I parted with every particle of property I had to my creditors, keeping only the clothes I wore on that day, my original drawings, and my gun, and without a dollar in my pocket, walked to Louisville alone."

This he speaks of as the saddest of all his journeys—"the only time in my life when the wild turkeys that so often crossed my path, and the thousands of lesser birds that enlivened the woods and the prairies, all looked like enemies, and I turned my eyes from them, as if I could have wished that they had never existed."

But the thought of his beloved Lucy and her children soon spurred him to action. He was a good draughtsman, he had been a pupil of David, he would turn his talents to account.

"As we were straightened to the very utmost, I undertook to draw portraits at the low price of five dollars per head, in black chalk. I drew a few gratis, and succeeded so well that ere many days had elapsed I had an abundance of work."

His fame spread, his orders increased. A settler came for him in the middle of the night from a considerable distance to have the portrait of his mother taken while she was on the eve of death, and a clergyman had his child's body exhumed that the artist might restore to him the lost features.

Money flowed in and he was soon again established with his family in a house in Louisville. His drawings of birds still continued and, he says, became at times almost a mania with him; he would frequently give up a head, the profits of which would have supplied the wants of his family a week or more, "to represent a little citizen of the feathered tribe."

In 1819 he was offered the position of taxidermist in the museum at Cincinnati, and soon moved there with his family. His pay not being forthcoming from the museum, he started a drawing school there, and again returned to his portraits. Without these resources, he says, he would have been upon the starving list. But food was plentiful and cheap. He writes in his journal: "Our living here is extremely moderate; the markets are well supplied and cheap, beef only two and one half cents a pound, and I am able to supply a good deal myself. Partridges are frequently in the streets, and I can shoot wild turkeys within a mile or so. Squirrels and Woodcock are very abundant in the season, and fish always easily caught."

In October, 1820, we again find him adrift, apparently with thought of having his bird drawings published, after he shall have further added to them by going through many of the southern and western states.

Leaving his family behind him, he started for New Orleans on a flatboat. He tarried long at Natchez, and did not reach the Crescent City till midwinter. Again he found himself destitute of means, and compelled to resort to portrait painting. He went on with his bird collecting and bird painting; in the meantime penetrating the swamps and bayous around the city.

At this time he seems to have heard of the publication of Wilson's "Ornithology," and tried in vain to get sight of a copy of it.

In the spring he made an attempt to get an appointment as draughtsman and naturalist to a government expedition that was to leave the next year to survey the new territory ceded to the United States by Spain. He wrote to President Monroe upon the subject, but the appointment never came to him. In March he called upon Vanderlyn, the historical painter, and took with him a portfolio of his drawings in hopes of getting a recommendation. Vanderlyn at first treated him as a mendicant and ordered him to leave his portfolio in the entry. After some delay, in company with a government official, he consented to see the pictures.

"The perspiration ran down my face," says Audubon, "as I showed him my drawings and laid them on the floor." He was thinking of the expedition to Mexico just referred to, and wanted to make a good impression upon Vanderlyn and the officer. This he succeeded in doing, and obtained from the artist a very complimentary note, as he did also from Governor Robertson of Louisiana.

In June, Audubon left New Orleans for Kentucky, to rejoin his wife and boys, but somewhere on the journey engaged himself to a Mrs. Perrie who lived at Bayou Sara, Louisiana, to teach her daughter drawing during the summer, at sixty dollars per month, leaving him half of each day to follow his own pursuits. He continued in this position till October when he took steamer for New Orleans. "My long, flowing hair, and loose yellow nankeen dress, and the unfortunate cut of my features, attracted much attention, and made me desire to be dressed like other people as soon as possible."

He now rented a house in New Orleans on Dauphine street, and determined to send for his family. Since he had left Cincinnati the previous autumn, he had finished sixty-two drawings of birds and plants, three quadrupeds, two snakes, fifty portraits of all sorts, and had lived by his talents, not having had a dollar when he started. "I sent a draft to my wife, and began life in New Orleans with forty-two dollars, health, and much eagerness to pursue my plan of collecting all the birds of America."

His family, after strong persuasion, joined him in December, 1821, and his former life of drawing portraits, giving lessons, painting birds, and wandering about the country, began again. His earnings proving inadequate to support the family, his wife took a position as governess in the family of a Mr. Brand.

In the spring, acting upon the judgment of his wife, he concluded to leave New Orleans again, and to try his fortunes elsewhere. He paid all his bills and took steamer for Natchez, paying his passage by drawing a crayon portrait of the captain and his wife.

On the trip up the Mississippi, two hundred of his bird portraits were sorely damaged by the breaking of a bottle of gunpowder in the chest in which they were being conveyed.

Three times in his career he met with disasters to his drawings. On the occasion of his leaving Hendersonville to go to Philadelphia, he had put two hundred of his original drawings in a wooden box and had left them in charge of a friend. On his return, several months later, he pathetically recounts what befell them: "A pair of Norway rats had taken possession of the whole, and reared a young family among gnawed bits of paper, which but a month previous, represented nearly one thousand inhabitants of the air!"

This discovery resulted in insomnia, and a fearful heat in the head; for several days he seemed like one stunned, but his youth and health stood him in hand, he rallied, and, undaunted, again sallied forth to the woods with dog and gun. In three years' time his portfolio was again filled.

The third catastrophe to some of his drawings was caused by a fire in a New York building in which his treasures were kept during his sojourn in Europe.

Audubon had an eye for the picturesque in his fellow-men as well as for the picturesque in Nature. On the Levee in New Orleans, he first met a painter whom he thus describes: "His head was covered by a straw hat, the brim of which might cope with those worn by the fair sex in 1830; his neck was exposed to the weather; the broad frill of a shirt, then fashionable, flopped about his breast, whilst an extraordinary collar, carefully arranged, fell over the top of his coat. The latter was of a light green colour, harmonising well with a pair of flowing yellow nankeen trousers, and a pink waistcoat, from the bosom of which, amidst a large bunch of the splendid flowers of the magnolia, protruded part of a young alligator, which seemed more anxious to glide through the muddy waters of a swamp than to spend its life swinging to and fro amongst folds of the finest lawn. The gentleman held in one hand a cage full of richly-plumed nonpareils, whilst in the other he sported a silk umbrella, on which I could plainly read 'Stolen from I,' these words being painted in large white characters. He walked as if conscious of his own importance; that is, with a good deal of pomposity, singing, 'My love is but a lassie yet'; and that with such thorough imitation of the Scotch emphasis that had not his physiognomy suggested another parentage, I should have believed him to be a genuine Scot. A narrower acquaintance proved him to be a Yankee; and anxious to make his acquaintance, I desired to see his birds. He retorted, 'What the devil did I know about birds?' I explained to him that I was a naturalist, whereupon he requested me to examine his birds. I did so with much interest, and was preparing to leave, when he bade me come to his lodgings and see the remainder of his collection. This I willingly did, and was struck with amazement at the appearance of his studio. Several cages were hung about the walls, containing specimens of birds, all of which I examined at my leisure. On a large easel before me stood an unfinished portrait, other pictures hung about, and in the room were two young pupils; and at a glance I discovered that the eccentric stranger was, like myself, a naturalist and an artist. The artist, as modest as he was odd, showed me how he laid on the paint on his pictures, asked after my own pursuits, and showed a friendly spirit which enchanted me. With a ramrod for a rest, he prosecuted his work vigorously, and afterwards asked me to examine a percussion lock on his gun, a novelty to me at the time. He snapped some caps, and on my remarking that he would frighten his birds, he exclaimed, 'Devil take the birds, there are more of them in the market.' He then loaded his gun, and wishing to show me that he was a marksman, fired at one of the pins on his easel. This he smashed to pieces, and afterward put a rifle bullet exactly through the hole into which the pin fitted."

Audubon reached Natchez on March 24, 1822, and remained there and in the vicinity till the spring of 1823, teaching drawing and French to private pupils and in the college at Washington, nine miles distant, hunting, and painting the birds, and completing his collection. Among other things he painted the "Death of Montgomery" from a print. His friends persuaded him to raffle the picture off. This he did, and taking one number himself, won the picture, while his finances were improved by three hundred dollars received for the tickets. Early in the autumn his wife again joined him, and presently we find her acting as governess in the home of a clergyman named Davis.

In December, there arrived in Natchez a wandering portrait painter named Stein, who gave Audubon his first lessons in the use of oil colours, and was instructed by Audubon in turn in chalk drawing.

There appear to have been no sacrifices that Mrs. Audubon was not willing and ready to make to forward the plans of her husband. "My best friends," he says at this time, "solemnly regarded me as a mad man, and my wife and family alone gave me encouragement. My wife determined that my genius should prevail, and that my final success as an ornithologist should be triumphant."

She wanted him to go to Europe, and, to assist toward that end, she entered into an engagement with a Mrs. Percy of Bayou Sara, to instruct her children, together with her own, and a limited number of outside pupils.

Audubon, in the meantime, with his son Victor, and his new artist friend, Stein, started off in a wagon, seeking whom they might paint, on a journey through the southern states. They wandered as far as New Orleans, but Audubon appears to have returned to his wife again in May, and to have engaged in teaching her pupils music and drawing. But something went wrong, there was a misunderstanding with the Percys, and Audubon went back to Natchez, revolving various schemes in his head, even thinking of again entering upon mercantile pursuits in Louisville.

He had no genius for accumulating money nor for keeping it after he had gotten it. One day when his affairs were at a very low ebb, he met a squatter with a tame black wolf which took Audubon's fancy. He says that he offered the owner a hundred dollar bill for it on the spot, but was refused. He probably means to say that he would have offered it had he had it. Hundred dollar bills, I fancy, were rarer than tame black wolves in that pioneer country in those days.

About this time he and his son Victor were taken with yellow fever, and Mrs. Audubon was compelled to dismiss her school and go to nurse them. They both recovered, and, in October (1823), set out for Louisville, making part of the journey on foot. The following winter was passed at Shipping Port, near Louisville, where Audubon painted birds, landscapes, portraits and even signs. In March he left Shipping Port for Philadelphia, leaving his son Victor in the counting house of a Mr. Berthoud. He reached Philadelphia on April 5, and remained there till the following August, studying painting, exhibiting his birds, making many new acquaintances, among them Charles Lucien Bonaparte, giving lessons in drawing at thirty dollars per month, all the time casting wistful eyes toward Europe, whither he hoped soon to be able to go with his drawings. In July he made a pilgrimage to Mill Grove where he had passed so many happy years. The sight of the old familiar scenes filled him with the deepest emotions.

In August he left Philadelphia for New York, hoping to improve his finances, and, may be, publish his drawings in that city. At this time he had two hundred sheets, and about one thousand birds. While there he again met Vanderlyn and examined his pictures, but says that he was not impressed with the idea that Vanderlyn was a great painter.

The birds that he saw in the museum in New York appeared to him to be set up in unnatural and constrained attitudes. With Dr. De Kay he visited the Lyceum, and his drawings were examined by members of the Institute. Among them he felt awkward and uncomfortable. "I feel that I am strange to all but the birds of America," he said. As most of the persons to whom he had letters of introduction were absent, and as his spirits soon grew low, he left on the fifteenth for Albany. Here he found his money low also. Abandoning the idea of visiting Boston, he took passage on a canal boat for Rochester. His fellow-passengers on the boat were doubtful whether he was a government officer, commissioner, or spy. At that time Rochester had only five thousand inhabitants. After a couple of days he went on to Buffalo and, he says, wrote under his name at the hotel this sentence: "Who, like Wilson, will ramble, but never, like that great man, die under the lash of a bookseller."

He visited Niagara, and gives a good account of the impressions which the cataract made upon him. He did not cross the bridge to Goat Island on account of the low state of his funds. In Buffalo he obtained a good dinner of bread and milk for twelve cents, and went to bed cheering himself with thoughts of other great men who had encountered greater hardships and had finally achieved fame.

He soon left Buffalo, taking a deck passage on a schooner bound for Erie, furnishing his own bed and provisions and paying a fare of one dollar and a half. From Erie he and a fellow-traveller hired a man and cart to take them to Meadville, paying their entertainers over night with music and portrait drawing. Reaching Meadville, they had only one dollar and a half between them, but soon replenished their pockets by sketching some of the leading citizens.

Audubon's belief in himself helped him wonderfully. He knew that he had talents, he insisted on using them. Most of his difficulties came from trying to do the things he was not fitted to do. He did not hesitate to use his talents in a humble way, when nothing else offered—portraits, landscapes, birds and animals he painted, but he would paint the cabin walls of the ship to pay his passage, if he was short of funds, or execute crayon portraits of a shoemaker and his wife, to pay for shoes to enable him to continue his journeys. He could sleep on a steamer's deck, with a few shavings for a bed, and, wrapped in a blanket, look up at the starlit sky, and give thanks to a Providence that he believed was ever guarding and guiding him.

Early in September he left for Pittsburg where he spent one month scouring the country for birds and continuing his drawings. In October, he was on his way down the Ohio in a skiff, in company with "a doctor, an artist and an Irishman." The weather was rainy, and at Wheeling his companions left the boat in disgust. He sold his skiff and continued his voyage to Cincinnati in a keel boat. Here he obtained a loan of fifteen dollars and took deck passage on a boat to Louisville, going thence to Shipping Port to see his son Victor. In a few days he was off for Bayou Sara to see his wife, and with a plan to open a school there.

"I arrived at Bayou Sara with rent and wasted clothes, and uncut hair, and altogether looking like the Wandering Jew."

In his haste to reach his wife and child at Mr. Percy's, a mile or more distant through the woods, he got lost in the night, and wandered till daylight before he found the house.

He found his wife had prospered in his absence, and was earning nearly three thousand dollars a year, with which she was quite ready to help him in the publication of his drawings. He forthwith resolved to see what he could do to increase the amount by his own efforts. Receiving an offer to teach dancing, he soon had a class of sixty organised. But the material proved so awkward and refractory that the master in his first lesson broke his bow and nearly ruined his violin in his excitement and impatience. Then he danced to his own music till the whole room came down in thunders of applause. The dancing lessons brought him two thousand dollars; this sum, together with his wife's savings, enabled him to foresee a successful issue to his great ornithological work.

On May, 1826, he embarked at New Orleans on board the ship *Delos* for Liverpool. His journal kept during this voyage abounds in interesting incidents and descriptions. He landed at Liverpool, July 20, and delivered some of his letters of introduction. He soon made the acquaintance of Mr. Rathbone, Mr. Roscoe, Mr. Baring, and Lord Stanley. Lord Stanley said in looking over his drawings: "This work is unique, and deserves the patronage of the Crown." In a letter to his wife at this time, Audubon said: "I am cherished by the most notable people in and around Liverpool, and have obtained letters of introduction to Baron Humboldt, Sir Walter Scott, Sir Humphry Davy, Sir Thomas Lawrence, Hannah More, Miss Edgeworth, and your distinguished cousin, Robert Bakewell." Mark his courtesy to his wife in this gracious mention of her relative—a courtesy which never forsook him—a courtesy which goes far toward retaining any woman's affection.

His paintings were put on exhibition in the rooms of the Royal Institution, an admittance of one shilling being charged. From this source he soon realised a hundred pounds.

He then went to Edinburgh, carrying letters of introduction to many well known literary and scientific men, among them Francis Jeffrey and "Christopher North."

Professor Jameson, the Scotch naturalist, received him coldly, and told him, among other things, that there was no chance of his seeing Sir Walter Scott—he was too busy. "*Not see Sir Walter Scott*?" thought I; "I SHALL, if I have to crawl on all fours for a mile." On his way up in the stage coach he had passed near Sir Walter's seat, and had stood up and craned his neck in vain to get a glimpse of the home of a man to whom, he says, he was indebted for so much pleasure. He and Scott were in many ways kindred spirits, men native to the open air, inevitable sportsmen, copious and romantic lovers and observers of all forms and conditions of life. Of course he will want to see Scott, and Scott will want to see him, if he once scents his real quality.

Later, Professor Jameson showed Audubon much kindness and helped to introduce him to the public.

In January, the opportunity to see Scott came to him.

"*January 22, Monday*. I was painting diligently when Captain Hall came in, and said: 'Put on your coat, and come with me to Sir Walter Scott; he wishes to see you *now*.' In a moment I was ready, for I really believe my coat and hat came to me instead of my going to them. My heart trembled; I longed for the meeting, yet wished it over. Had not his wondrous pen penetrated my soul with the consciousness that here was a genius from God's hand? I felt overwhelmed at the thought of meeting Sir Walter, the Great Unknown. We reached the house, and a powdered waiter was asked if Sir Walter were in. We were shown forward at once, and entering a very small room Captain Hall said: 'Sir Walter, I have brought Mr. Audubon.' Sir Walter came forward, pressed my hand warmly, and said he was 'glad to have the honour of meeting me.' His long, loose, silvery locks struck me; he looked like Franklin at his best. He also reminded me of Benjamin West; he had the great benevolence of William Roscoe about him and a kindness most prepossessing. I could not forbear looking at him, my eyes feasted on his countenance. I watched his movements as I would those of a celestial being; his long, heavy, white eyebrows struck me forcibly. His little room was tidy, though it partook a good deal of the character of a laboratory. He was wrapped in a quilted morning-gown of light purple silk; he had been at work writing on the 'Life of Napoleon.' He writes close lines, rather curved as they go from left to right, and puts an immense deal on very little paper. After a few minutes had elapsed, he begged Captain Hall to ring a bell; a servant came and was asked to bid Miss Scott come to see Mr. Audubon. Miss Scott came, black haired and black-dressed, not handsome but said to be highly accomplished, and she is the daughter of Sir Walter Scott. There was much conversation. I talked but little, but, believe me, I listened and observed, careful if ignorant. I cannot write more now. I have just returned from the Royal Society. Knowing that I was a candidate for the electorate of the society, I felt very uncomfortable and would gladly have been hunting on Tawapatee Bottom."

It may be worth while now to see what Scott thought of Audubon. Under the same date, Sir Walter writes in his journal as follows: "*January* 22, 1827. A visit from Basil Hall, with Mr. Audubon, the ornithologist, who has followed the pursuit by many a long wandering in the American forests. He is an American by naturalisation, a Frenchman by birth; but less of a Frenchman than I have ever seen—no dust or glimmer, or shine about him, but great simplicity of manners and behaviour; slight in person and plainly dressed; wears long hair, which time has not yet tinged; his countenance acute, handsome, and interesting, but still simplicity is the predominant characteristic. I wish I had gone to see his drawings; but I had heard so much about them that I resolved not to see them—'a crazy way of mine, your honour.'"

Two days later Audubon again saw Scott, and writes in his journal as follows: "*January* 24. My second visit to Sir Walter Scott was much more agreeable than my first. My portfolio and its contents were matters on which I could speak substantially, and I found him so willing to level himself with me for awhile that the time spent at his home was agreeable and valuable. His daughter improved in looks the moment she spoke, having both vivacity and good sense."

Scott's impressions of the birds as recorded in his journal, was that the drawings were of the first order, but he thought that the aim at extreme correctness and accuracy made them rather stiff.

In February Audubon met Scott again at the opening of the Exhibition at the rooms of the Royal Institution.

"*Tuesday, February* 13. This was the grand, long promised, and much wished-for day of the opening of the Exhibition at the rooms of the Royal Institution. At one o'clock I went, the doors were just opened, and in a few minutes the rooms were crowded. Sir Walter Scott was present; he came towards me, shook my hand cordially, and pointing to Landseer's picture said: 'Many such scenes, Mr. Audubon, have I witnessed in my younger days.' We talked much of all about us, and I would gladly have joined him in a glass of wine, but my foolish habits prevented me, and after inquiring of his daughter's health, I left him, and shortly afterwards the rooms; for I had a great appetite, and although there were tables loaded with delicacies, and I saw the ladies particularly eating freely, I must say to my shame I dared not lay my fingers on a single thing. In the evening I went to the theatre where I was much amused by 'The Comedy of Errors,' and afterwards, 'The Green Room.' I admire Miss Neville's singing very much; and her manners also; there is none of the actress about her, but much of the lady."

Audubon somewhere says of himself that he was "temperate to an intemperate degree"—the accounts in later years show that he became less strict in this respect. He would not drink with Sir Walter Scott at this time, but he did with the Texan Houston and with President Andrew Jackson, later on.

In September we find him exhibiting his pictures in Manchester, but without satisfactory results. In the lobby of the exchange where his pictures were on exhibition, he overheard one man say to another: "Pray, have you seen Mr. Audubon's collection of birds? I am told it is well worth a shilling; suppose we go now."

"Pah! it is all a hoax; save your shilling for better use. I have seen them; the fellow ought to be drummed out of town."

In 1827, in Edinburgh, he seems to have issued a prospectus for his work, and to have opened books of subscription, and now a publisher, Mr. Lizars, offers to bring out the first number of "Birds of America," and on November 28, the first proof of the first engraving was shown him, and he was pleased with it.

With a specimen number he proposed to travel about the country in quest of subscribers until he had secured three hundred. In his journal under date of December 10, he says: "My success in Edinburgh borders on the miraculous. My book is to be published in numbers containing four [in another place he says five] birds in each, the size of life, in a style surpassing anything now existing, at two guineas a number. The engravings are truly beautiful; some of them have been coloured, and are now on exhibition."

Audubon's journal, kept during his stay in Edinburgh, is copious, graphic, and entertaining. It is a mirror of everything he saw and felt.

Among others he met George Combe, the phrenologist, author of the once famous *Constitution of Man*, and he submitted to having his head "looked at." The examiner said: "There cannot exist a moment of doubt that this gentleman is a painter, colourist, and compositor, and, I would add, an amiable though quick tempered man."

Audubon was invited to the annual feast given by the Antiquarian Society at the Waterloo Hotel, at which Lord Elgin presided. After the health of many others had been drunk, Audubon's was proposed by Skene, a Scottish historian. "Whilst he was engaged in a handsome panegyric, the perspiration poured from me. I thought I should faint." But he survived the ordeal and responded in a few appropriate words. He was much dined and wined, and obliged to keep late hours—often getting no more than four hours sleep, and working hard painting and writing all the next day. He often wrote in his journals for his wife to read later, bidding her Good-night, or rather Good-morning, at three A.M.

Audubon had the bashfulness and awkwardness of the backwoodsman, and doubtless the naiveté and picturesqueness also; these traits and his very great merits as a painter of wild life, made him a favourite in Edinburgh society. One day he went to read a paper on the Crow to Dr. Brewster, and was so nervous and agitated that he had to pause for a moment in the midst of it. He left the paper with Dr. Brewster and when he got it back again was much shocked: "He had greatly improved the style (for I had none), but he had destroyed the matter."

During these days Audubon was very busy writing, painting, receiving callers, and dining out. He grew very tired of it all at times, and longed for the solitude of his native woods. Some days his room was a perfect levee. "It is Mr. Audubon here, and Mr. Audubon there; I only hope they will not make a conceited fool of Mr. Audubon at last." There seems to have been some danger of this, for he says: "I seem in a measure to have gone back to my early days of society and fine dressing, silk stockings and pumps, and all the finery with which I made a popinjay of myself in my youth.... I wear my hair as long as usual, I believe it does as much for me as my paintings."

He wrote to Thomas Sully of Philadelphia, promising to send him his first number, to be presented to the Philadelphia Society—"an institution which thought me unworthy to be a member," he writes.

About this time he was a guest for a day or two of Earl Morton, at his estate Dalmahoy, near Edinburgh. He had expected to see an imposing personage in the great Chamberlain to the late queen Charlotte. What was his relief and surprise, then, to see a "small, slender man, tottering on his feet, weaker than a newly hatched partridge," who welcomed him with tears in his eyes. The countess, "a fair, fresh-complexioned woman, with dark, flashing eyes," wrote her name in his subscription book, and offered to pay the price in advance. The next day he gave her a lesson in drawing.

On his return to Edinburgh he dined with Captain Hall, to meet Francis Jeffrey. "Jeffrey is a little man," he writes, "with a serious face and dignified air. He looks both shrewd and cunning, and talks with so much volubility he is rather displeasing.... Mrs. Jeffrey was nervous and very much dressed."

Early in January he painted his "Pheasant attacked by a Fox." This was his method of proceeding: "I take one [a fox] neatly killed, put him up with wires, and when satisfied with the truth of the position, I take my palette and work as rapidly as possible; the same with my birds. If practicable, I finish the bird at one sitting,—often, it is true, of fourteen hours,—so that I think they are correct, both in detail and in composition."

In pictures by Landseer and other artists which he saw in the galleries of Edinburgh, he saw the skilful painter, "the style of men who know how to handle a brush, and carry a good effect," but he missed that closeness and fidelity to Nature which to him so much outweighed mere technique. Landseer's "Death of a Stag" affected him like a farce. It was pretty, but not real and true. He did not feel that way about the sermon he heard Sydney Smith preach: "It was a sermon to *me*. He made me smile and he made me think deeply. He pleased me at times by painting my foibles with due care, and again I felt the colour come to my cheeks as he portrayed my sins." Later, he met Sydney Smith and his "fair daughter," and heard the latter sing. Afterwards he had a note from the famous divine upon which he remarks: "The man should study economy; he would destroy more paper in a day than Franklin would in a week; but all great men are more or less eccentric. Walter Scott writes a diminutive hand, very difficult to read, Napoleon a large scrawling one, still more difficult, and Sydney Smith goes up hill all the way with large strides."

Having decided upon visiting London, he yielded to the persuasions of his friends and had his hair cut before making the trip. He chronicles the event in his journal as a very sad one, in which "the will of God was usurped by the wishes of man." Shorn of his locks he probably felt humbled like the stag when he loses his horns.

Quitting Edinburgh on April 5, he visited, in succession, Newcastle, Leeds, York, Shrewsbury, and Manchester, in quest of subscribers to his great work. A few were obtained at each place at two hundred pounds per head. At Newcastle he first met Bewick, the famous wood engraver, and conceived a deep liking for him.

We find him in London on May 21, 1827, and not in a very happy frame of mind: "To me London is just like the mouth of an immense monster, guarded by millions of sharp-edged teeth, from which, if I escape unhurt, it must be called a miracle." It only filled him with a strong desire to be in his beloved woods again. His friend, Basil Hall, had insisted upon his procuring a black suit of clothes. When he put this on to attend his first dinner party, he spoke of himself as "attired like a mournful raven," and probably more than ever wished himself in the woods.

He early called upon the great portrait painter, Sir Thomas Lawrence, who inspected his drawings, pronounced them "very clever," and, in a few days, brought him several purchasers for some of his animal paintings, thus replenishing his purse with nearly one hundred pounds.

Considering Audubon's shy disposition, and his dread of persons in high places, it is curious that he should have wanted to call upon the King, and should have applied to the American Minister, Mr. Gallatin, to help him to do so. Mr. Gallatin laughed and said: "It is impossible, my dear sir, the King sees nobody; he has the gout, is peevish, and spends his time playing whist at a shilling a rubber. I had to wait six weeks before I was presented to him in my position of ambassador." But his work was presented to the King who called it fine, and His Majesty became a subscriber on the usual terms. Other noble persons followed suit, yet Audubon was despondent. He had removed the publication of his work from Edinburgh to London, from the hands of Mr. Lizars into those of Robert Havell. But the enterprise did not prosper, his agents did not attend to business, nor to his orders, and he soon found himself at bay for means to go forward with the work. At this juncture he determined to make a sortie for the purpose of collecting his dues and to add to his subscribers. He visited Leeds, York, and other towns. Under date of October 9, at York, he writes in his journal: "How often I thought during these visits of poor Alexander Wilson. Then travelling as I am now, to procure subscribers he, as well as myself, was received with rude coldness, and sometimes with that arrogance which belongs to *parvenus.*"

A week or two later we find him again in Edinburgh where he breakfasted with Professor Wilson ("Christopher North"), whom he greatly enjoyed, a man without stiffness or ceremonies: "No cravat, no waistcoat, but a fine frill of his own profuse beard, his hair flowing uncontrolled, and his speech dashing at once at the object in view, without circumlocution.... He gives me comfort by being comfortable himself."

In early November he took the coach for Glasgow, he and three other passengers making the entire journey without uttering a single word: "We sat like so many owls of different species, as if afraid of one another." Four days in Glasgow and only one subscriber.

Early in January he is back in London arranging with Mr. Havell for the numbers to be engraved in 1828. One day on looking up to the new moon he saw a large flock of wild ducks passing over, then presently another flock passed. The sight of these familiar objects made him more homesick than ever. He often went to Regent's Park to see the trees, and the green grass, and to hear the sweet notes of the black birds and starlings.

The black birds' note revived his drooping spirits: to his wife he writes, "it carries my mind to the woods around thee, my Lucy."

Now and then a subscriber withdrew his name, which always cut him to the quick, but did not dishearten him.

"*January 28*. I received a letter from D. Lizars to-day announcing to me the loss of four subscribers; but these things do not dampen my spirits half so much as the smoke of London. I am as dull as a beetle."

In February he learned that it was Sir Thomas Lawrence who prevented the British Museum from subscribing to his work: "He considered the drawings so-so, and the engraving and colouring bad; when I remember how he praised these same drawings *in my presence*, I wonder—that is all."

The rudest man he met in England was the Earl of Kinnoul: "A small man with a face like the caricature of an owl." He sent for Audubon to tell him that all his birds were alike, and that he considered his work a swindle. "He may really think this, his knowledge is probably small; but it is not the custom to send for a gentleman to abuse him in one's own house." Audubon heard his words, bowed and left him without speaking.

In March he went to Cambridge and met and was dined by many learned men. The University, through its Librarian, subscribed for his work. Other subscriptions followed. He was introduced to a judge who wore a wig that "might make a capital bed for an Osage Indian during the whole of a cold winter on the Arkansas River."

On his way to Oxford he saw them turn a stag from a cart "before probably a hundred hounds and as many huntsmen. A curious land, and a curious custom, to catch an animal and then set it free merely to catch it again." At Oxford he received much attention, but complains that not one of the twenty-two colleges subscribed for his work, though two other institutions did.

Early in April we find him back in London lamenting over his sad fate in being compelled to stay in so miserable a place. He could neither write nor draw to his satisfaction amid the "bustle, filth, and smoke." His mind and heart turned eagerly toward America, and to his wife and boys, and he began seriously to plan for a year's absence from England. He wanted to renew and to improve about fifty of his drawings. During this summer of 1828, he was very busy in London, painting, writing, and superintending the colouring of his plates. Under date of August 9, he writes in his journal: "I have been at work from four every morning until dark; I have kept up my large correspondence. My publication goes on well and regularly, and this very day seventy sets have been distributed, yet the number of my subscribers has not increased; on the contrary, I have lost some." He made the acquaintance of Swainson, and the two men found much companionship in each other, and had many long talks about birds: "Why, Lucy, thou wouldst think that birds were all that we cared for in this world, but thou knowest this is not so."

Together he and Mr. and Mrs. Swainson planned a trip to Paris, which they carried out early in September. It tickled Audubon greatly to find that the Frenchman at the office in Calais, who had never seen him, had described his complexion in his passport as copper red, because he was an American, all Americans suggesting aborigines. In Paris they early went to call upon Baron Cuvier. They were told that he was too busy to be seen: "Being determined to look at the Great Man, we waited, knocked again, and with a certain degree of firmness, sent in our names. The messenger returned, bowed, and led the way up stairs, where in a minute Monsieur le Baron, like an excellent good man, came to us. He had heard much of my friend Swainson, and greeted him as he deserves to be greeted; he was polite and kind to me, though my name had never made its way to his ears. I looked at him and here follows the result: Age about sixty-five; size corpulent, five feet five English measure; head large, face wrinkled and brownish; eyes grey, brilliant and sparkling; nose aquiline, large and red; mouth large with good lips; teeth few, blunted by age, excepting one on the lower jaw, *measuring nearly three-quarters of an inch square.*" The italics are not Audubon's. The great naturalist invited his callers to dine with him at six on the next Saturday.

They next presented their letter to Geoffroy de St. Hilaire, with whom they were particularly pleased. Neither had he ever heard of Audubon's work. The dinner with Cuvier gave him a nearer view of the manners and habits of the great man. "There was not the show of opulence at this dinner that is seen in the same rank of life in England, no, not by far, but it was a good dinner served *à la Française.*" Neither was it followed by the "drinking matches" of wine, so common at English tables.

During his stay in Paris Audubon saw much of Cuvier, and was very kindly and considerately treated by him. One day he accompanied a portrait painter to his house and saw him sit for his portrait: "I see the Baron now, quite as plainly as I did this morning,—an old green surtout about him, a neckcloth that would have wrapped his whole body if unfolded, loosely tied about his chin, and his silver locks looking like those of a man who loves to study books better than to visit barbers."

Audubon remained in Paris till near the end of October, making the acquaintance of men of science and of artists, and bringing his work to the attention of those who were likely to value it. Baron Cuvier reported favourably upon it to the Academy of Sciences, pronouncing it "the most magnificent monument which has yet been erected to ornithology." He obtained thirteen subscribers in France and spent forty pounds.

On November 9, he is back in London, and soon busy painting, and pressing forward the engraving and colouring of his work. The eleventh number was the first for the year 1829.

The winter was largely taken up in getting ready for his return trip to America. He found a suitable agent to look after his interests, collected some money, paid all his debts, and on April 1 sailed from Portsmouth in the packet ship *Columbia*. He was sea-sick during the entire voyage, and reached New York May 5. He did not hasten to his family as would have been quite natural after so long an absence, but spent the summer and part of the fall in New Jersey and Pennsylvania, prosecuting his studies and drawings of birds, making his headquarters in Camden, New Jersey. He spent six weeks in the Great Pine Forest, and much time at Great Egg Harbor, and has given delightful accounts of these trips in his journals. Four hours' sleep out of the twenty-four was his allotted allowance.

One often marvels at Audubon's apparent indifference to his wife and his home, for from the first he was given to wandering. Then, too, his carelessness in money matters, and his improvident ways, necessitating his wife's toiling to support the family, put him in a rather unfavourable light as a "good provider," but a perusal of his journal shows that he was keenly alive to all the hardships and sacrifices of his wife, and from first to last in his journeyings he speaks of his longings for home and family. "Cut off from all dearest me," he says in one of his youthful journeys, and in his latest one he speaks of himself as being as happy as one can be who is "three thousand miles from the dearest friend on earth." Clearly some impelling force held him to the pursuit of this work, hardships or no hardships. Fortunately for him, his wife shared his belief in his talents and in their ultimate recognition.

Under date of October 11, 1829, he writes: "I am at work and have done much, but I wish I had eight pairs of hands, and another body to shoot the specimens; still I am delighted at what I have accumulated in drawings this season. Forty-two drawings in four months, eleven large, eleven middle size, and twenty-two small, comprising ninety-five birds, from eagles downwards, with plants, nests, flowers, and sixty different kinds of eggs. I live alone, see scarcely anyone besides those belonging to the house where I lodge. I rise long before day, and work till nightfall, when I take a walk and to bed."

Audubon's capacity for work was extraordinary. His enthusiasm and perseverance were equally extraordinary. His purposes and ideas fairly possessed him. Never did a man consecrate himself more fully to the successful completion of the work of his life, than did Audubon to the finishing of his "American Ornithology."

During this month Audubon left Camden and turned his face toward his wife and children, crossing the mountains to Pittsburg in the mail coach with his dog and gun, thence down the Ohio in a steamboat to Louisville, where he met his son Victor, whom he had not seen for five years. After a few days here with his two boys, he started for Bayou Sara to see his wife. Beaching Mr. Johnson's house in the early morning, he went at once to his wife's apartment: "Her door was ajar, already she was dressed and sitting by her piano, on which a young lady was playing. I pronounced her name gently, she saw me, and the next moment I held her in my arms. Her emotion was so great I feared I had acted rashly, but tears relieved our hearts, once more we were together."

Mrs. Audubon soon settled up her affairs at Bayou Sara, and the two set out early in January, 1830, for Louisville, thence to Cincinnati, thence to Wheeling, and so on to Washington, where Audubon exhibited his drawings to the House of Representatives and received their subscriptions as a body. In Washington, he met the President, Andrew Jackson, and made the acquaintance of Edward Everett. Thence to Baltimore where he obtained three more subscribers, thence to New York from which port he sailed in April with his wife on the packet ship Pacific, for England, and arrived at Liverpool in twenty-five days.

This second sojourn in England lasted till the second of August, 1831. The time was occupied in pushing the publication of his "Birds," canvassing the country for new subscribers, painting numerous pictures for sale, writing his "Ornithological Biography," living part of the time in Edinburgh, and part of the time in London, with two or three months passed in France, where there were fourteen subscribers. While absent in America, he had been elected a fellow of the Royal Society of London, and on May 6 took his seat in the great hall.

He needed some competent person to assist him in getting his manuscript ready for publication and was so fortunate as to obtain the services of MacGillivray, the biographer of British Birds.

Audubon had learned that three editions of Wilson's "Ornithology" were soon to be published in Edinburgh, and he set to work vigorously to get his book out before them. Assisted by MacGillivray, he worked hard at his biography of the birds, writing all day, and Mrs. Audubon making a copy of the work to send to America to secure copyright there. Writing to her sons at this time, Mrs. Audubon says: "Nothing is heard but the steady movement of the pen; your father is up and at work before dawn, and writes without ceasing all day."

When the first volume was finished, Audubon offered it to two publishers, both of whom refused it, so he published it himself in March, 1831.

In April on his way to London he travelled "on that Extraordinary road called the railway, at the rate of twenty-four miles an hour."

The first volume of his bird pictures was completed this summer, and, in bringing it out, forty thousand dollars had passed through his hands. It had taken four years to bring that volume before the world, during which time no less than fifty of his subscribers, representing the sum of fifty-six thousand dollars, had abandoned him, so that at the end of that time, he had only one hundred and thirty names standing on his list.

It was no easy thing to secure enough men to pledge themselves to $1,000 for a work, the publication of which must of necessity extend over eight or ten years.

Few enterprises, involving such labour and expense, have ever been carried through against such odds.

The entire cost of the "Birds" exceeded one hundred thousand dollars, yet the author never faltered in this gigantic undertaking.

On August 2, Audubon and his wife sailed for America, and landed in New York on September 4. They at once went to Louisville where the wife remained with her sons, while the husband went to Florida where the winter of 1831-2 was spent, prosecuting his studies of our birds. His adventures and experiences in Florida, he has embodied in his Floridian Episodes, "The Live Oakers," "Spring Garden," "Deer Hunting," "Sandy Island," "The Wreckers," "The Turtles," "Death of a Pirate," and other sketches. Stopping at Charleston, South Carolina, on this southern trip, he made the acquaintance of the Reverend John Bachman, and a friendship between these two men was formed that lasted as long as they both lived. Subsequently, Audubon's sons, Victor and John, married Dr. Bachman's two eldest daughters.

In the summer of 1832, Audubon, accompanied by his wife and two sons, made a trip to Maine and New Brunswick, going very leisurely by private conveyance through these countries, studying the birds, the people, the scenery, and gathering new material for his work. His diaries give minute accounts of these journeyings. He was impressed by the sobriety of the people of Maine; they seem to have had a "Maine law" at that early date; "for on asking for brandy, rum, or whiskey, not a drop could I obtain." He saw much of the lumbermen and was a deeply interested spectator of their ways and doings. Some of his best descriptive passages are contained in these diaries.

In October he is back in Boston planning a trip to Labrador, and intent on adding more material to his "Birds" by another year in his home country.

That his interests abroad in the meantime might not suffer by being entirely in outside hands, he sent his son Victor, now a young man of considerable business experience, to England to represent him there. The winter of 1832 and 1833 Audubon seems to have spent mainly in Boston, drawing and re-drawing and there he had his first serious illness.

In the spring of 1833, a schooner was chartered and, accompanied by five young men, his youngest son, John Woodhouse, among them, Audubon started on his Labrador trip, which lasted till the end of summer. It was an expensive and arduous trip, but was greatly enjoyed by all hands, and was fruitful in new material for his work. Seventy-three bird skins were prepared, many drawings made, and many new plants collected.

The weather in Labrador was for the most part rainy, foggy, cold, and windy, and his drawings were made in the cabin of his vessel, often under great difficulties. He makes this interesting observation upon the Eider duck: "In one nest of the Eider ten eggs were found; this is the most we have seen as yet in any one nest. The female draws the down from her abdomen as far toward her breast as her bill will allow her to do, but the feathers are not pulled, and on examination of several specimens, I found these well and regularly planted, and cleaned from their original down, as a forest of trees is cleared of its undergrowth. In this state the female is still well clothed, and little or no difference can be seen in the plumage, unless examined."

He gives this realistic picture of salmon fishermen that his party saw in Labrador: "On going to a house on the shore, we found it a tolerably good cabin, floored, containing a good stove, a chimney, and an oven at the bottom of this, like the ovens of the French peasants, three beds, and a table whereon the breakfast of the family was served. This consisted of coffee in large bowls, good bread, and fried salmon. Three Labrador dogs came and sniffed about us, and then returned under the table whence they had issued, with no appearance of anger. Two men, two women, and a babe formed the group, which I addressed in French. They were French-Canadians and had been here several years, winter and summer, and are agents for the Fur and Fish Co., who give them food, clothes, and about $80 per annum. They have a cow and an ox, about an acre of potatoes planted in sand, seven feet of snow in winter, and two-thirds less salmon than was caught here ten years since. Then, three hundred barrels was a fair season; now one hundred is the maximum; this is because they will catch the fish both ascending and descending the river. During winter the men hunt Foxes, Martens, and Sables, and kill some bear of the black kind, but neither Deer nor other game is to be found without going a great distance in the interior, where Reindeer are now and then procured. One species of Grouse, and one of Ptarmigan, the latter white at all seasons; the former, I suppose to be, the Willow Grouse. The men would neither sell nor give us a single salmon, saying, that so strict were their orders that, should they sell *one,* the place might be taken from them. If this should prove the case everywhere, I shall not purchase many for my friends. The furs which they collect are sent off to Quebec at the first opening of the waters in spring, and not a skin of any sort was here for us to look at."

He gives a vivid picture of the face of Nature in Labrador on a fine day, under date of July 2: "A beautiful day for Labrador. Drew another *M. articus.* Went on shore, and was most pleased with what I saw. The country, so wild and grand, is of itself enough to interest any one in its wonderful dreariness. Its mossy, grey-clothed rocks, heaped and thrown together as if by chance, in the most fantastical groups imaginable, huge masses hanging on minor ones as if about to roll themselves down from their doubtful-looking situations, into the depths of the sea beneath. Bays without end, sprinkled with rocky islands of all shapes and sizes, where in every fissure a Guillemot, a Cormorant, or some other wild bird retreats to secure its egg, and raise its young, or save itself from the hunter's pursuit. The peculiar cast of the sky, which never seems to be certain, butterflies flitting over snowbanks, probing beautiful dwarf flowerets of many hues, pushing their tender, stems from the thick bed of moss which everywhere covers the granite rocks. Then the morasses, wherein you plunge up to your knees, or the walking over the stubborn, dwarfish shrubbery, making one think that as he goes he treads down the *forests* of Labrador. The unexpected Bunting, or perhaps Sylvia, which, perchance, and indeed as if by chance alone, you now and then see flying before you, or hear singing from the creeping plants on the ground. The beautiful freshwater lakes, on the rugged crests of greatly elevated islands, wherein the Red and Black-necked Divers swim as proudly as swans do in other latitudes, and where the fish appear to have been cast as strayed beings from the surplus food of the ocean. All—all is wonderfully grand, wild—aye, and terrific. And yet how beautiful it is now, when one sees the wild bee, moving from one flower to another in search of food, which doubtless is as sweet to it, as the essence of the magnolia is to those of favoured Louisiana. The little Ring Plover rearing its delicate and tender young, the Eider Duck swimming man-of-war-like amid her floating brood, like the guardship of a most valuable convoy; the White-crowned Bunting's sonorous note reaching the ear ever and anon; the crowds of sea birds in search of places wherein to repose or to feed—how beautiful is all this in this wonderful rocky desert at this season, the beginning of July, compared with the horrid blasts of winter which here predominate by the will of God, when every rock is rendered smooth with snows so deep that every step the traveller takes is as if entering into his grave; for even should he escape an avalanche, his eye dreads to search the horizon, for full well he knows that snow—snow is all that can be seen. I watched the Ring Plover for some time; the parents were so intent on saving their young that they both lay on the rocks as if shot, quivering their wings and dragging their bodies as if quite disabled. We left them and their young to the care of the Creator. I would not have shot one of the old ones, or taken one of the young for any consideration, and I was glad my young men were as forbearing. The *L. marinus* is extremely abundant here; they are forever harassing every other bird, sucking their eggs, and devouring their young; they take here the place of Eagles and Hawks; not an Eagle have we seen yet, and only two or three small Hawks, and one small Owl; yet what a harvest they would have here, were there trees for them to rest upon."

On his return from Labrador in September, Audubon spent three weeks in New York, after which with his wife, he started upon another southern trip, pausing at Philadelphia, Baltimore, Washington, and Richmond. In Washington he made some attempts to obtain permission to accompany a proposed expedition to the Rocky Mountains, under Government patronage. But the cold and curt manner in which Cass, then Secretary of War, received his application, quite disheartened him. But he presently met Washington Irving, whose friendly face and cheering words revived his spirits. How one would like a picture of that meeting in Washington between Audubon and Irving—two men who in so many ways were kindred spirits!

Charleston, South Carolina, was reached late in October, and at the home of their friend Bachman the Audubons seem to have passed the most of the winter of 1833-4: "My time was well employed; I hunted for new birds or searched for more knowledge of old. I drew, I wrote many long pages. I obtained a few new subscribers, and made some collections on account of my work."

His son Victor wrote desiring the presence of his father in England, and on April 16, we find him with his wife and son John, again embarked for Liverpool. In due time they are in London where they find Victor well, and the business of publication going on prosperously. One of the amusing incidents of this sojourn, narrated in the diaries, is Audubon's and his son's interview with the Baron Rothschild, to whom he had a letter of introduction from a distinguished American banking house. The Baron was not present when they entered his private office, but "soon a corpulent man appeared, hitching up his trousers, and a face red with the exertion of walking, and without noticing anyone present, dropped his fat body into a comfortable chair, as if caring for no one else in this wide world but himself. While the Baron sat, we stood, with our hats held respectfully in our hands. I stepped forward, and with a bow tendered my credentials. 'Pray, sir,' said the man of golden consequence, 'is this a letter of business, or is it a mere letter of introduction?' This I could not well answer, for I had not read the contents of it, and I was forced to answer rather awkwardly, that I could not tell. The banker then opened the letter, read it with the manner of one who was looking only at the temporal side of things, and after reading it said, 'This is only a letter of introduction, and I expect from its contents that you are the publisher of some book or other and need my subscription.'

"Had a man the size of a mountain spoken to me in that arrogant style in America, I should have indignantly resented it; but where I then was it seemed best to swallow and digest it as well as I could. So in reply to the offensive arrogance of the banker, I said I should be *honoured* by his subscription to the "Birds of America." 'Sir,' he said, 'I never sign my name to any subscription list, but you may send in your work and I will pay for a copy of it. Gentlemen, I am busy. I wish you good morning.' We were busy men, too, and so bowing respectfully, we retired, pretty well satisfied with the small slice of his opulence which our labour was likely to obtain.

"A few days afterwards I sent the first volume of my work half bound, and all the numbers besides, then published. On seeing them we were told that he ordered the bearer to take them to his house, which was done directly. Number after number was sent and delivered to the Baron, and after eight or ten months my son made out his account and sent it by Mr. Havell, my engraver, to his banking-house. The Baron looked at it with amazement, and cried out, 'What, a hundred pounds for birds! Why, sir, I will give you five pounds and not a farthing more!' Representations were made to him of the magnificence and expense of the work, and how pleased his Baroness and wealthy children would be to have a copy; but the great financier was unrelenting. The copy of the work was actually sent back to Mr. Havell's shop, and as I found that instituting legal proceedings against him would cost more than it would come to, I kept the work, and afterwards sold it to a man with less money but a nobler heart. What a distance there is between two such men as the Baron Rothschild of London, and the merchant of Savannah!"

Audubon remained in London during the summer of 1834, and in the fall removed to Edinburgh, where he hired a house and spent a year and a half at work on his "Ornithological Biography," the second and third volumes of which were published during that time.

In the summer of 1836, he returned to London, where he settled his family in Cavendish Square, and in July, with his son John, took passage at

Portsmouth for New York, desiring to explore more thoroughly the southern states for new material for his work. On his arrival in New York, Audubon, to his deep mortification, found that all his books, papers, and valuable and curious things, which he had collected both at home and abroad, had been destroyed in the great fire in New York, in 1835.

In September he spent some time in Boston where he met Brewer and Nuttall, and made the acquaintance of Daniel Webster, Judge Story, and others.

Writing to his son in England, at this time, admonishing him to carry on the work, should he himself be taken away prematurely, he advises him thus: "Should you deem it wise to remove the publication of the work to this country, I advise you to settle in Boston; *I have faith in the Bostonians."*

In Salem he called upon a wealthy young lady by the name of Silsby, who had the eyes of a gazelle, but "when I mentioned subscription it seemed to fall on her ears, not as the cadence of the wood thrush, or of the mocking bird does on mine, but as a shower bath in cold January."

From Boston Audubon returned in October to New York, and thence went southward through Philadelphia to Washington, carrying with him letters from Washington Irving to Benjamin F. Butler, then the Attorney General of the United States, and to Martin Van Buren who had just been elected to the presidency. Butler was then quite a young man: "He read Washington Irving's letter, laid it down, and began a long talk about his talents, and after a while came round to my business, saying that the Government allows so little money to the departments, that he did not think it probable that their subscription could be obtained without a law to that effect from Congress."

At this time he also met the President, General Jackson: "He was very kind, and as soon as he heard that we intended departing to-morrow evening for Charleston, invited us to dine with him *en famille.* At the hour named we went to the White House, and were taken into a room, where the President soon joined us, I sat close to him; we spoke of olden times, and touched slightly on politics, and I found him very averse to the Cause of the Texans.... The dinner was what might be called plain and substantial in England; I dined from a fine young turkey, shot within twenty miles of Washington. The General drank no wine, but his health was drunk by us more than once; and he ate very moderately; his last dish consisting of bread and milk."

In November Audubon is again at the house of his friend Dr. Bachman, in Charleston, South Carolina. Here he passed the winter of 1836-7, making excursions to various points farther south, going as far as Florida. It was at this time that he seems to have begun, in connection with Dr. Bachman, his studies in Natural History which resulted in the publication, a few years later, of the "Quadrupeds of North America."

In the spring he left Charleston and set out to explore the Gulf of Mexico, going to Galveston and thence well into Texas, where he met General Sam Houston. Here is one of his vivid, realistic pen pictures of the famous Texan: "We walked towards the President's house, accompanied by the Secretary of the Navy, and as soon as we rose above the bank, we saw before us a level of far-extending prairie, destitute of timber, and rather poor soil. Houses half finished, and most of them without roofs, tents, and a liberty pole, with the capitol, were all exhibited to our view at once. We approached the President's mansion, however, wading through water above our ankles. This abode of President Houston is a small log house, consisting of two rooms, and a passage through, after the southern fashion. The moment we stepped over the threshold, on the right hand of the passage we found ourselves ushered into what in other countries would be called the antechamber; the ground floor, however, was muddy and filthy, a large fire was burning, a small table covered with paper and writing materials, was in the centre, camp-beds, trunks, and different materials, were strewed about the room. We were at once presented to several members of the cabinet, some of whom bore the stamp of men of intellectual ability, simple, though bold, in their general appearance. Here we were presented to Mr. Crawford, an agent of the British Minister to Mexico, who has come here on some secret mission.

"The President was engaged in the opposite room on some national business, and we could not see him for some time. Meanwhile we amused ourselves by walking to the capitol, which was yet without a roof, and the floors, benches, and tables of both houses of Congress were as well saturated with water as our clothes had been in the morning. Being invited by one of the great men of the place to enter a booth to take a drink of grog with him, we did so; but I was rather surprised that he offered his name, instead of the cash to the bar-keeper.

"We first caught sight of President Houston as he walked from one of the grog shops, where he had been to prevent the sale of ardent spirits. He was on his way to his house, and wore a large grey coarse hat; and the bulk of his figure reminded me of the appearance of General Hopkins of Virginia, for like him he is upwards of six feet high, and strong in proportion. But I observed a scowl in the expression of his eyes, that was forbidding and disagreeable. We reached his abode before him, but he soon came, and we were presented to his excellency. He was dressed in a fancy velvet coat, and trousers trimmed with broad gold lace; around his neck was tied a cravat somewhat in the style of seventy-six. He received us kindly, was desirous of retaining us for awhile, and offered us every facility within his power. He at once removed us from the ante-room to his private chamber, which, by the way, was not much cleaner than the former. We were severally introduced by him to the different members of his cabinet and staff, and at once asked to drink grog with him, which we did, wishing success to his new republic. Our talk was short: but the impression which was made on my mind at the time by himself, his officers, and his place of abode, can never be forgotten."

Late in the summer of 1837, Audubon, with his son John and his new wife—the daughter of Dr. Bachman, returned to England for the last time. He finally settled down again in Edinburgh and prepared the fourth volume of his "Ornithological Biography." This work seems to have occupied him a year. The volume was published in November, 1838. More drawings for his "Birds of America" were finished the next winter, and also the fifth volume of the "Biography" which was published in May, 1839.

In the fall of that year the family returned to America and settled in New York City, at 86 White street. His great work, the "Birds of America," had been practically completed, incredible difficulties had been surmounted, and the goal of his long years of striving had been reached. About one hundred and seventy-five copies of his "Birds" had been delivered to subscribers, eighty of the number in this country.

In a copy of the "Ornithological Biography" given in 1844 by Audubon to J. Prescott Hall, the following note, preserved in the *Magazine of American History* (1877) was written by Mr. Hall. It is reproduced here in spite of its variance from statements now accepted:—

"Mr. Audubon told me in the year 184- that he did not sell more than 40 copies of his great work in England, Ireland, Scotland and France, of which Louis Philippe took 10.

"The following received their copies but never paid for them: George IV., Duchess of Clarence, Marquis of Londonderry, Princess of Hesse Homburg.

"An Irish lord whose name he would not give, took two copies and paid for neither. Rothschild paid for his copy, but with great reluctance.

"He further said that he sold 75 copies in America, 26 in New York and 24 in Boston; that the work cost him £27,000 and that he lost $25,000 by it.

"He said that Louis Philippe offered to subscribe for 100 copies if he would publish the work in Paris. This he found could not be done, as it would have required 40 years to finish it as things were then in Paris. Of this conversation I made a memorandum at the time which I read over to Mr. Audubon and he pronounced it correct.

"J. PRESCOTT HALL."

IV

About the very great merit of this work, there is but one opinion among competent judges. It is, indeed, a monument to the man's indomitable energy and perseverance, and it is a monument to the science of ornithology. The drawings of the birds are very spirited and life like, and their biographies copious, picturesque, and accurate, and, taken in connection with his many journals, they afford glimpses of the life of the country during the early part of the century, that are of very great interest and value.

In writing the biography of the birds he wrote his autobiography as well; he wove his doings and adventures into his natural history observations. This gives a personal flavour to his pages, and is the main source of their charm.

His account of the Rosebreasted Grosbeak is a good sample of his work in this respect:

"One year, in the month of August, I was trudging along the shores of the Mohawk river, when night overtook me. Being little acquainted with that part of the country, I resolved to camp where I was; the evening was calm and beautiful, the sky sparkled with stars which were reflected by the smooth waters, and the deep shade of the rocks and trees of the opposite shore fell on the bosom of the stream, while gently from afar came on the ear the muttering sound of the cataract. My little fire was soon lighted under a rock, and, spreading out my scanty stock of provisions, I reclined on my grassy couch. As I looked on the fading features of the beautiful landscape, my heart turned towards my distant home, where my friends were doubtless wishing me, as I wish them, a happy night and peaceful slumbers. Then were heard the barkings of the watch dog, and I tapped my faithful companion to prevent his answering them. The thoughts of my worldly mission then came over my mind, and having thanked the Creator of all for his never-failing mercy, I closed my eyes, and was passing away into the world of dreaming existence, when suddenly there burst on my soul the serenade of the Rosebreasted bird, so rich, so mellow, so loud in the stillness of the night, that sleep fled from my eyelids. Never did I enjoy music more: it thrilled through my heart, and surrounded me with an atmosphere of bliss. One might easily have imagined that even the Owl, charmed by such delightful music, remained reverently silent. Long after the sounds ceased did I enjoy them, and when all had again become still, I stretched out my wearied limbs, and gave myself up to the luxury of repose."

Probably most of the seventy-five or eighty copies of "Birds" which were taken by subscribers in this country are still extant, held by the great libraries, and learned institutions. The Lenox Library in New York owns three sets. The Astor Library owns one set. I have examined this work there; there are four volumes in a set; they are elephant folio size—more than three feet long, and two or more feet wide. They are the heaviest books I ever handled. It takes two men to carry one volume to the large racks which hold them for the purpose of examination. The birds, of which there are a thousand and fifty-five specimens in four hundred and thirty-five plates, are all life size, even the great eagles, and appear to be unfaded. This work, which cost the original subscribers one thousand dollars, now brings four thousand dollars at private sale.

Of the edition with reduced figures and with the bird biographies, many more were sold, and all considerable public libraries in this country possess the work. It consists of seven imperial octavo volumes. Five hundred dollars is the average price which this work brings. This was a copy of the original English publication, with the figures reduced and lithographed. In this work, his sons, John and Victor, greatly assisted him, the former doing the reducing by the aid of the camera-lucida, and the latter attending to the printing and publishing. The first volume of this work appeared in 1840, and the last in 1844.

Audubon experimented a long time before he hit upon a satisfactory method of drawing his birds. Early in his studies he merely drew them in outline. Then he practised using threads to raise the head, wing or tail of his specimen. Under David he had learned to draw the human figure from a manikin. It now occurred to him to make a manikin of a bird, using cork or wood, or wires for the purpose. But his bird manikin only excited the laughter and ridicule of his friends. Then he conceived the happy thought of setting up the body of the dead bird by the aid of wires, very much as a taxidermist mounts them. This plan worked well and enabled him to have his birds permanently before him in a characteristic attitude: "The bird fixed with wires on squares I studied as a lay figure before me, its nature previously known to me as far as habits went, and its general form having been perfectly observed."

His bird pictures reflect his own temperament, not to say his nationality; the birds are very demonstrative, even theatrical and melodramatic at times. In some cases this is all right, in others it is all wrong. Birds differ in this respect as much as people do—some are very quiet and sedate, others pose and gesticulate like a Frenchman. It would not be easy to exaggerate, for instance, the flashings and evolutions of the redstart when it arrives in May, or the acting and posing of the catbird, or the gesticulations of the yellow breasted chat, or the nervous and emphatic character of the large-billed water thrush, or the many pretty attitudes of the great Carolina wren; but to give the same dramatic character to the demure little song sparrow, or to the slow moving cuckoo, or to the pedestrian cowbird, or to the quiet Kentucky warbler, as Audubon has done, is to convey a wrong impression of these birds.

Wilson errs, if at all, in the other direction. His birds, on the other hand, reflect his cautious, undemonstrative Scotch nature. Few of them are shown in violent action like Audubon's cuckoo; their poses for the most part are easy and characteristic. His drawings do not show the mastery of the subject and the versatility that Audubon's do;—they have not the artistic excellence, but they less frequently do violence to the bird's character by exaggerated activity.

The colouring in Audubon's birds is also often exaggerated. His purple finch is as brilliant as a rose, whereas at its best, this bird is a dull carmine.

Either the Baltimore oriole has changed its habits of nest-building since Audubon's day, or else he was wrong in his drawing of the nest of that bird, in making the opening on the side near the top. I have never seen an oriole's nest that was not open at the top.

In his drawings of a group of robins, one misses some of the most characteristic poses of that bird, while some of the attitudes that are portrayed are not common and familiar ones.

But in the face of all that he accomplished, and against such odds, and taking into consideration also the changes that may have crept in through engraver and colourists, it ill becomes us to indulge in captious criticisms. Let us rather repeat Audubon's own remark on realising how far short his drawings came of representing the birds themselves: "After all, there's nothing perfect but *primitiveness*."

Finding that he could not live in the city, in 1842 Audubon removed with his family to "Minnie's Land," on the banks of the Hudson, now known as Audubon Park, and included in the city limits; this became his final home.

In the spring of 1843 he started on his last long journey, his trip to the Yellow-stone River, of which we have a minute account in his "Missouri River Journals"—documents that lay hidden in the back of an old secretary from 1843 to the time when they were found by his grand-daughters in 1896, and published by them in 1897.

This trip was undertaken mainly in the interests of the "Quadrupeds and Biography of American Quadrupeds," and much of what he saw and did is woven into those three volumes. The trip lasted eight months, and the hardships and exposures seriously affected Audubon's health. He returned home in October, 1843.

He was now sixty-four or five years of age, and the infirmities of his years began to steal upon him.

The first volume of his "Quadrupeds" was published about two years later, and this was practically his last work. The second and third volumes were mainly the work of his sons, John and Victor.

The "Quadrupeds" does not take rank with his "Birds." It was not his first love. It was more an after thought to fill up his time. Neither the drawing nor the colouring of the animals, largely the work of his son John, approaches those of the birds.

"Surely no man ever had better helpers" says his grand-daughter, and a study of his life brings us to the same conclusion—his devoted wife, his able and willing sons, were his closest helpers, nor do we lose sight of the assistance of the scientific and indefatigable MacGillivray, and the untiring and congenial co-worker, Dr. Bachman.

Audubon's last years were peaceful and happy, and were passed at his home on the Hudson, amid his children and grandchildren, surrounded by the scenes that he loved.

After his eyesight began to fail him, his devoted wife read to him, she walked with him, and toward the last she fed him. "Bread and milk were his breakfast and supper, and at noon he ate a little fish or game, never having eaten animal food if he could avoid it."

One visiting at the home of our naturalist during his last days speaks of the tender way in which he said to his wife: "Well, sweetheart, always busy. Come sit thee down a few minutes and rest."

Parke Godwin visited Audubon in 1846, and gives this account of his visit:

"The house was simple and unpretentious in its architecture, and beautifully embowered amid elms and oaks. Several graceful fawns, and a noble elk, were stalking in the shade of the trees, apparently unconscious of the presence of a few dogs, and not caring for the numerous turkeys, geese, and other domestic animals that gabbled and screamed around them. Nor did my own approach startle the wild, beautiful creatures, that seemed as docile as any of their tame companions.

"'Is the master at home?' I asked of a pretty maid servant, who answered my tap at the door; and who, after informing me that he was, led me into a room on the left side of the broad hall. It was not, however, a parlour, or an ordinary reception room that I entered, but evidently a room for work. In one corner stood a painter's easel, with the half-finished sketch of a beaver on the paper; in the other lay the skin of an American panther. The antlers of elks hung upon the walls; stuffed birds of every description of gay plumage ornamented the mantel-piece; and exquisite drawings of field mice, orioles, and woodpeckers, were scattered promiscuously in other parts of the room, across one end of which a long, rude table was stretched to hold artist materials, scraps of drawing paper, and immense folio volumes, filled with delicious paintings of birds taken in their native haunts.

"'This,' said I to myself, 'is the studio of the naturalist,' but hardly had the thought escaped me when the master himself made his appearance. He was a tall thin man, with a high-arched and serene forehead, and a bright penetrating grey eye; his white locks fell in clusters upon his shoulders, but were the only signs of age, for his form was erect, and his step as light as that of a deer. The expression of his face was sharp, but noble and commanding, and there was something in it, partly derived from the aquiline nose and partly from the shutting of the mouth, which made you think of the imperial eagle.

"His greeting as he entered, was at once frank and cordial, and showed you the sincere true man. 'How kind it is,' he said, with a slight French accent and in a pensive tone, 'to come to see me; and how wise, too, to leave that crazy city.' He then shook me warmly by the hand. 'Do you know,' he continued, 'how I wonder that men can consent to swelter and fret their lives away amid those hot bricks and pestilent vapours, when the woods and fields are all so near? It would kill me soon to be confined in such a prison house; and when I am forced to make an occasional visit there, it fills me with loathing and sadness. Ah! how often, when I have been abroad on the mountains, has my heart risen in grateful praise to God that it was not my destiny to waste and pine among those noisome congregations of the city.'"

Another visitor to Audubon during his last days writes: "In my interview with the naturalist, there were several things that stamped themselves indelibly on my mind. The wonderful simplicity of the man was perhaps the most remarkable. His enthusiasm for facts made him unconscious of himself. To make him happy you had only to give him a new fact in natural history, or introduce him to a rare bird. His self-forgetfulness was very impressive. I felt that I had found a man who asked homage for God and Nature, and not for himself.

"The unconscious greatness of the man seemed only equalled by his child-like tenderness. The sweet unity between his wife and himself, as they turned over the original drawings of his birds, and recalled the circumstances of the drawings, some of which had been made when she was with him; her quickness of perception, and their mutual enthusiasm regarding these works of his heart and hand, and the tenderness with which they unconsciously treated each other, all was impressed upon my memory. Ever since, I have been convinced that Audubon owed more to his wife than the world knew, or ever would know. That she was always a reliance, often a help, and ever a sympathising sister-soul to her noble husband, was fully apparent to me."

One notes much of the same fire and vigour in the later portraits of Audubon, that are so apparent in those of him in his youthful days. What a resolute closing of the mouth in his portrait taken of him in his old age—"the magnificent grey-haired man!"

In 1847, Audubon's mind began to fail him; like Emerson in his old age, he had difficulty in finding the right word.

In May, 1848, Dr. Bachman wrote of him: "My poor friend Audubon! The outlines of his beautiful face and form are there, but his noble mind is all in ruins."

His feebleness increased (there was no illness), till at sunset, January 27, 1851, in his seventy-sixth year, the "American Woodsman," as he was wont to call himself, set out on his last long journey to that bourne whence no traveller returns.

V

As a youth Audubon was an unwilling student of books; as a merchant and mill owner in Kentucky he was an unwilling man of business, but during his whole career, at all times and in all places, he was more than a willing student of ornithology—he was an eager and enthusiastic one. He brought to the pursuit of the birds, and to the study of open air life generally, the keen delight of the sportsman, united to the ardour of the artist moved by beautiful forms.

He was not in the first instance a man of science, like Cuvier, or Agassiz, or Darwin—a man seeking exact knowledge; but he was an artist and a backwoodsman, seeking adventure, seeking the gratification of his tastes, and to put on record his love of the birds. He was the artist of the birds before he was their historian; the writing of their biographies seems to have been only secondary with him.

He had the lively mercurial temperament of the Latin races from which he sprang. He speaks of himself as "warm, irascible, and at times violent."

His perceptive powers, of course, led his reflective. His sharpness and quickness of eye surprised even the Indians. He says: "My *observatory nerves* never gave way."

His similes and metaphors were largely drawn from the animal world. Thus he says, "I am as dull as a beetle," during his enforced stay in London. While he was showing his drawings to Mr. Rathbone, he says: "I was panting like the winged pheasant." At a dinner in some noble house in England he said that the men servants "moved as quietly as killdeers." On another occasion, when the hostess failed to put him at his ease: "There I stood, motionless as a Heron."

With all his courage and buoyancy, Audubon was subject to fits of depression, probably the result largely of his enforced separation from his family. On one occasion in Edinburgh he speaks of these attacks, and refers pathetically to others he had had: "But that was in beloved America, where the ocean did not roll between me and my wife and sons."

Never was a more patriotic American. He loved his adopted country above all other lands in which he had journeyed.

Never was a more devoted husband, and never did wife more richly deserve such devotion than did Mrs. Audubon. He says of her: "She felt the pangs of our misfortune perhaps more heavily than I, but never for an hour lost her courage; her brave and cheerful spirit accepted all, and no reproaches from her beloved lips ever wounded my heart. With her was I not always rich?"

"The waiting time, my brother, is the hardest time of all."

While Audubon was waiting for better luck, or for worse, he was always listening to the birds and studying them—storing up the knowledge that he turned to such good account later: but we can almost hear his neighbours and acquaintances calling him an "idle, worthless fellow." Not so his wife; she had even more faith in him than he had in himself.

His was a lovable nature—he won affection and devotion easily, and he loved to be loved; he appreciated the least kindness shown him.

He was always at ease and welcome in the squatter's cabin or in elegantly appointed homes, like that of his friends, the Rathbones, though he does complain of an awkwardness and shyness sometimes when in high places. This, however, seemed to result from the pomp and ceremony found there, and not because of the people themselves.

"Chivalrous, generous, and courteous to his heart's core," says his granddaughter, "he could not believe others less so, till painful experiences taught him; then he was grieved, hurt, but never embittered; and, more marvellous yet, with his faith in his fellows as strong as ever, again and again he subjected himself to the same treatment."

On one occasion when his pictures were on exhibition in England, some one stole one of his paintings, and a warrant was issued against a deaf mute. "Gladly would I have painted a bird for the poor fellow," said Audubon, "and I certainly did not want him arrested."

He was never, even in his most desperate financial straits, too poor to help others more poor than himself.

He had a great deal of the old-fashioned piety of our fathers, which crops out abundantly in his pages. While he was visiting a Mr. Bently in Manchester, and after retiring to his room for the night, he was surprised by a knock at his door. It appeared that his host in passing thought he heard Audubon call to him to ask for something: "I told him I prayed aloud every night, as had been my habit from a child at my mother's knees in Nantes. He said nothing for a moment, then again wished me good night and was gone."

Audubon belonged to the early history of the country, to the pioneer times, to the South and the West, and was, on the whole, one of the most winsome, interesting, and picturesque characters that have ever appeared in our annals.

BIBLIOGRAPHY

[Footnote: Note: This bibliography is that of the original 1902 edition. Many books on Audubon have been published since then.]

The works of Audubon are mentioned in the chronology at the beginning of the volume and in the text. Of the writings about him the following—apart from the obvious books of reference in American biography—are the main sources of information:—

I. PROSE WRITINGS OF AMERICA. By Rufus Wilmot Griswold. (Philadelphia, 1847: Carey & Hart.)

II. BRIEF BIOGRAPHIES. By Samuel Smiles. (Boston, 1861: Ticknor & Fields.)

III. AUDUBON, THE NATURALIST OF THE NEW WORLD: His ADVENTURES AND DISCOVERIES. By Mrs. Horace Roscoe Stebbing St. John. (Revised, with additions. Boston, 1864: Crosby & Nichols. New York, 1875: The World Publishing House.)

IV. THE LIFE AND ADVENTURES OF JOHN JAMES AUDUBON, THE NATURALIST. Edited, from materials supplied by his widow, by Robert Buchanan. (London, 1868: S. Low, son & Marston.)

V. THE LIFE OF JOHN JAMES AUDUBON. Edited by his widow, with an Introduction by James Grant Wilson. (New York, 1869: Putnams.)

VI. FAMOUS MEN OF SCIENCE. By Sarah Knowles Bolton. (Boston, 1889: T. Y. Crowell & Co.)

VII. AUDUBON AND HIS JOURNALS. By Maria R. Audubon. With Zoological and Other Notes by Elliott Coues. (New York, 1897: Charles Scribner's Sons. Two volumes.) This is by far the most interesting and authentic of any of the sources of information.